SEGREGATION AND THE BIBLE

SEGREGATION
and the
BIBLE

EVERETT TILSON

ABINGDON PRESS

NEW YORK   NASHVILLE

SEGREGATION AND THE BIBLE

Copyright © MCMLVIII by Abingdon Press

Library of Congress Catalog Card Number: 58-7437

SET UP, PRINTED, AND BOUND BY THE
PARTHENON PRESS, AT NASHVILLE,
TENNESSEE, UNITED STATES OF AMERICA

To the members of the congregation of the St. Peter's Presbyterian Church, Spencertown, New York, who, because they treasure vital Christian fellowship more highly than personal or denominational distinctions, have rekindled the hope of Mary and me for the Church of our children, Stephen, Lee, Hazel, and Joe.

PREFACE

MOST DISCUSSIONS OF THE QUESTION OF THE RELATIONSHIP OF
the Bible to the current racial crisis revolve around one or the
other of three questions. Does the Bible, as a few churchmen
passionately contend, demand segregation? Or does it record
precedents, as many churchmen believe, that can be construed as
props with which to support the general principle of segregation?
Or as a still much larger number of churchmen are prone to ask
or at least wonder, just what are the implications of basic biblical
faith, if any, for the Christian approach to this crucial problem
in human relations?

In this book I try to suggest tentative answers to these three
questions. In Chapters I–III I evaluate the arguments of those
who give an affirmative answer to the first of these questions.
And I strive to do so within the framework of the assumptions
about the nature and use of the scriptures on which such arguments seem to rest.

In Chapters IV–VI I do much the same for those who answer
the second of the above questions in the affirmative. But these
chapters, due largely to the very nature of the question to which
they are addressed, contain some rather definite implications,
as do not appear in the preceding chapters, for the Christian
approach to this whole problem. At least they do if we are at all
inclined to take seriously the faith and practice of Christ and

the apostles. And few of us, I trust, feel disposed to take them lightly, even though we will probably not be able to reproduce either in every detail.

In Chapters VII–IX I delineate some of the implications of biblical faith for our whole approach to the issue of segregation. But I make no attempt to translate these suggestions into a specific program for our churches. I try merely to illuminate some of the guiding principles for facing this matter from the vantage point of the biblical perspective. And I narrow the scope of my task for an altogether simple reason. I do so from the conviction that our great need in this area is not for more and better answers. Most of us already have an ample supply of good answers to questions concerning race. Of this fact we have no doubt. Indeed we are likely to be a little proud of the confidence we have in the correctness of our answers—so proud, in fact, as to view the whole matter as a closed case or, if as an open case, with a closed mind. Our really crucial need is for a greater and nobler faith. Even a faith that calls in question our answers will scarcely suffice. It must also be a faith sufficiently great and noble to call in question the pride with which we have cherished these answers.

Biblical quotations follow the King James Version.

Several friends have assisted me in various ways in the preparation of this study. Two people in particular, Howard A. Kester and J. Philip Hyatt, played decisive roles in kindling my interest in this project. Prof. Kester, until recently the executive secretary of the Fellowship of Southern Churchmen and now a member of the faculty of Eureka College, first suggested the need for a book in this area. Then, at the suggestion of Dr. Hyatt, my colleague on the faculty of the Vanderbilt University Divinity

School, Mr. Kester asked me whether I would undertake such a study. I responded in the affirmative.

I hereby express my profound gratitude to the following persons for their helpful suggestions concerning matters of style and/or interpretation, on the basis of a critical reading of parts or all of the manuscript: Will D. Campbell, a Southern Baptist minister and the assistant director of the Department of Racial and Cultural Relations of the National Council of the Churches of Christ in the U.S.A.; Raymond T. Ferris, rector of Christ Episcopal Church of Nashville, Tennessee; Clyde C. Flannery, pastor of Brookmeade Congregational Church of Nashville, Tennessee; James D. Glasse, my colleague on the faculty of the Vanderbilt University Divinity School; Jameson Jones, a staff member of the Department of College and University Religious Life of the Division of Educational Institutions of the Board of Education of the Methodist Church; Howard A. Kester; James E. Sellers, assistant to the dean of the Vanderbilt University Divinity School; Lou H. Silberman and D. Bard Thompson, members of the faculty of the Vanderbilt University Divinity School; and Galen Weaver, secretary of racial and cultural relations of the Council for Christian Social Action for United Church of Christ.

I also acknowledge my deep appreciation to William C. Walzer, associate general director of the Joint Commission on Missionary Education of the National Council of the Churches of Christ in the U.S.A., a highly respected former teacher and close friend; and William J. Simmons, chaplain of Tennessee A. & I. State University, for their occasional reminders of the need for such a study.

To Mrs. Jameson Jones, Mrs. Harold Kieler, Mrs. Syd Oliver,

Mrs. David Adams, and Mrs. Evelyn Hay, I express my grateful appreciation for highly competent secretarial assistance.

To my wife Mary, who has controlled the interruptions from Steve, Lee, Hazel, and Joe throughout the course of my work on this project, I am most grateful.

EVERETT TILSON

CONTENTS

11

PART I

Does the Bible Demand Segregation?

Introduction

A SOUTHERN MINISTER CHOSE THE SUPREME COURT DECISION OUT-
lawing segregation in the public schools as the subject of an
article for one of the city's daily papers. "We should not have
been surprised," he wrote, "by this ruling. . . . Our democratic
philosophy . . . and our Christian teachings have always required
the interpretation the Supreme Court has now handed down. We
have all known it. We have all anticipated it. We . . . all . . .
knew our way was contrary to everything God has taught us." [1]

Two years later, in equally unequivocal language, a local lawyer
took exception to the above interpretation of that decision.
"Segregation," he declared, "predates the known history of the
world. God was the original segregationist. . . . The decision was
absolutely wrong." [2]

The spokesmen of these quite irreconciliable positions share
more things in common than a Southern address. Both have
been active in local political circles. Both have been influential
leaders in their respective churches. And neither cited the Scriptures in defense of his view.

How can two Christians with so much in common give exactly
opposite answers to so basic a question in human relations? Because of their failure, some would answer, to consult the Scriptures. Such persons might even document their charge with this
quotation from the Westminster Confession of Faith: "The
Supreme Judge, by which all controversies of religion are to be

15

determined, . . . and in whose sentence we are to rest, can be no other but the Holy Spirit speaking in the Scripture." [3] Therefore, if we want the right answer to this question, we can find it in short order. We have only to seek the guidance of the Holy Spirit in our perusal of the Bible. This, many Christians teach. This, many Christians believe.

So let us consider the words of two men who have sought the help of the Bible and, we trust, the guidance of the Holy Spirit in their study of this problem. Let us look first at the statement made by Albert C. Winn, chairman of the standing committee on Christian relations, in an address to the 1955 Presbyterian, U.S., General Assembly:

> Fathers and brethren, believe me it is not that I for some reason was opposed to segregation and have sought texts to support me in that position. I was raised in a segregated society in South Carolina. . . . In the same unconscious way I learned to be courteous to ladies, I was taught that the Negro had his place.
>
> It was the Word of God which convicted me. It was the Word of God which persuaded me that our mores are wrong here, that our customs are contrary to God's will.[4]

A minister of this same denomination, G. T. Gillespie, president emeritus of Belhaven College, Jackson, Mississippi, in an address before the Synod of Mississippi, came to exactly the opposite position as a result of his study of the Scriptures. Said he:

> While the Bible contains no clear mandate for or against segregation as between the white and negro races, it does furnish considerable data from which valid inferences may be drawn in support of the general principle of segregation as an important feature of . . . Divine purpose and Providence throughout the Ages.[5]

These conflicting statements clearly demonstrate that we cannot accept at face value a man's readiness to acknowledge the authority of the Bible as proof of guidance by the Holy Spirit. They indicate the need for another approach to this knotty problem of religious authority. Indeed we might well ask if a person's exegesis of the Scriptures does not provide us with an excellent check on his relationship with the Holy Spirit. When given a highly selective or palpably forced exegesis of Scriptures, should we not trace such defection to the prejudice of the interpreter of the Bible rather than the unreliability of the Holy Spirit as guide?

In the following pages we shall be comparing the respective claims of the segregationists and integrationists to the guidance of the Holy Spirit. And we shall do so on the basis of the methods and arguments which they allegedly deduce from the Bible in support of their respective positions. Does the Bible advocate segregation? Or if not, will it tolerate segregation? Or does it demand integration? And if so, when? These are some of the questions with which we shall be concerned in this study.

The Key Passages
from the Book of Genesis

WHAT ARE THE MINIMAL REQUIREMENTS FOR THE ADMISSION OF the Bible as a witness for the defense of the *status quo* in American race relations? A professional in research would doubtless require mention by name of the two dominant races in this country. "For the Bible to qualify as such a witness," he would probably say, "it must either expressly demand or clearly imply the elevation of all Caucasians and the subordination of all Negroes in every place and for all time."

Even a casual survey of the biblical defenses of segregation betrays the inability of the Bible to meet this initial requirement. Nor do the authors of such defenses hesitate to take other equally great liberties in their use of the Bible. For example, they characteristically equate segregation with separation,[1] and they exhibit little curiosity as to the grounds of the alleged separation. They even claim the demand of an ancient Jew for separation from all Gentiles as a biblical precedent for their position. They insist that this entitles their group of Gentiles— the Caucasians—to demand the segregation of another group of Gentiles—the Negroes. Thus they convert what originally was a plea for religious purity into a prop for the support of racial purity.[2]

The writers of such literature do not have a monopoly on this type of biblical interpretation. Many upstanding—and some

18

outstanding—Christians interpret the Bible similarly. Quite often, to be sure, their respect for the authority of the Bible somewhat exceeds their knowledge of its contents. Nevertheless, more than a few of them have been impressed by the above use of the Bible in support of segregation. And understandably so, for the average segregationist employs the Scriptures in a manner capable of imitation by the rank-and-file churchman.

This does not mean that many Christian bodies would entrust the definition of their doctrinal position to rank-and-file churchmen. But considering the influence of such churchmen in American religious life, we do well to examine the biblical passages which some of them have been led to interpret as supports for segregation. By the same token, we should do so from the standpoint of their rather uncritical approach to the Scriptures.

Let us begin this examination with a look at the Genesis passages which have been turned into props with which to shore up the cause of segregation. We shall group them according to the particular arguments for which they purportedly serve as the basis.

The Origin of Racial Boundaries

Segregationists hail the Genesis (9:18-29) account of the separation of peoples after the flood as proof of the divine origin of the segregation of the races. This story relates the division of the world among the sons of Noah. Gillespie comments on this passage as follows:

The descendants of Shem migrated eastward and occupied most of Asia; the descendants of Japheth migrated westward . . . and ultimately occupied the continent of Europe, while the children

19

of Ham moved . . . southward . . . and occupied the continent of Africa.

This brief record . . . , while affirming the unity of the race, also implies that an all-wise Providence . . . is . . . responsible for the distinct racial characteristics . . . which are chiefly responsible for the segregation of racial groups across the centuries and in our time.[3]

At least these two assumptions underlie Gillespie's use of this passage in support of segregation: (1) that Japheth, Ham, and Shem were the progenitors of distinct racial groups, (2) that all subsequent migrations of the descendants of these racial groups have been without divine sanction. What shall we say of these assumptions in the light of the Bible and world history?

The first of these assumptions is rooted in biological, linguistic, historical, and literary considerations of an extremely dubious nature. Though we are "still largely in ignorance of the exact ways in which biological processes work to form new physical types," [4] at least we can say this without fear of reproof: no reputable scientist has yet attempted to account for the origin of the three major racial groups within a single generation from a set of common parents. (Gen. 7:13.)[5] If possible, the linguistic argument rests on even flimsier grounds, presupposing as it does the knowledge of at least two Semitic languages[6] and a razor-sharp imagination. Nor does the historical argument fare any better. The treatment of this narrative as an explanation of the origin of the three major racial groups would not only require the recognition of Shem as the progenitor of the Mongoloid group, but it would also require the classification of the Jews as members of the Mongoloid rather than the white group. Need we say more of the impossibility of the historical aspect of this assumption? But the really devastating argument against

20

the use of this passage as a text for segregation is rooted in literary considerations. Specialists in the interpretation of biblical literature insist that the author of this narrative never intended or attempted to give us an account of the separation of men on the basis of their physical characteristics. Indeed, the writer very seldom takes note of racial differences at all, and then, significantly enough, not from the viewpoint of a racial purist, but from the viewpoint of the geographer.[7]

Let us look now at some of the subsequent migrations of these racial groups, and at a few of the population shifts we would have to maneuver in the implementation of a program of repatriation based on this alleged division of the races. Six million American Jews would have to be resettled in overcrowded Palestine; millions of Italian Americans would have to be removed to Europe; and the same goes for the Scotch-Irish Presbyterians— not to mention the Swedish Baptists or the Welsh Methodists. Then, multitudes of us would have to be strewn, bone by bone, over at least three continents.

Quite apart from the practical absurdity of this suggestion, its underlying assumption flatly contradicts the prophetic view of God's control over history. The prophets credit God with the direction of numerous population movements outside and beyond the geographical boundaries set in this particular chapter of Genesis. They betray no knowledge whatever of such a remote and static deity. Their God is a living, active deity, and whenever men try to lock him in their little national, geographical, or, for that matter, ecclesiastical corral, he breaks through the splintered gate to the tune of prophetic applause. And to do what? On more than one occasion it was either to lead the children of Israel, the descendants of Shem, into the continent of Africa, the inheritance of Ham and his descendants, or vice versa. In fact, the Shemites cannot even get out of the book of Genesis without the help of the hospitality of the Egyptians, designated in the Genesis table of nations as Hamitic descendants (Gen. 10:6). And in a rhetorical question to which the context rules out the possibility of a negative reply, Amos 9:7 invites consideration of the shocking possibility, "Are ye not as children of the Ethiopians [an Hamitic people] unto me, O children of Israel? saith the Lord. Have not I brought up Israel out of the land of Egypt? and the Philistines from Caphtor?" Then, lest the clear meaning of this question suffer misinterpretation at the hands of some ingenious exegete, the prophet proceeds to scatter the Israelites over the whole of the inhabitable earth. "For, lo, I will command," the prophet declares in the name of the Lord, "and I will sift the house of Israel among all nations, like as corn is sifted in a sieve" (9:9).

Two additional facts deserve consideration before we leave the analysis of this biblical provision for segregation. For one thing, as in the case of the distinctively Israelite view of history, it presupposes the control of history by a suprahistorical power. But the similarity between this and the distinctively Israelite view of history ends here, for, whereas the former derives its view of God from its knowledge of past tradition, the latter derives its view of past tradition from its knowledge of God. Then, as "the night the day," the advocates of this first view end up trying to show why we must remain where we are, though possibly not what or as we are, whether we like it or not. In effect, though they might refuse to admit as much, such persons feel as little need for an "Overruling Providence" as isolationists for the United Nations.

Now for the other point of interest in connection with this argument. The Bible presents several spokesmen of this view.

They gauge God's action in the present by his actions in the past. Once, such prophets outnumbered the prophetic spokesmen for a more dynamic view of God by four hundred to one (I Kings 22), but the people for whom the four hundred left their utterances boasted some very discriminating individuals. They did not admit the words of such prophets into the canon of Scriptures. Indeed, the Bible seldom mentions prophets of this type except in a derogatory manner. In fact, it almost never mentions them except in connection with their opposition to the prophets whose utterances were canonized. The Greek translation of the Old Testament makes this fact especially clear, for it does not refer to this type of religious functionary as a prophet (prophētēs). It calls him instead a "false prophet."

The Curse on Ham

A closely related argument, frequently employed in the nineteenth century in support of slavery, stems from God's alleged curse on Ham.[8] This curse appears as a sort of anticlimax to the story of Noah's conquest by wine. Reduced to a drunken stupor by his overindulgence in the fruit of the vine, Noah removes all his clothes, lies down in his tent, and goes to sleep. "And Ham," we read, "the father of Canaan, saw the nakedness of his father. . . . And Noah awoke from his wine, and knew what his younger son had done unto him. And he said, Cursed be Canaan; a servant of servants shall he be unto his brethren." (Gen. 9:22-25.)

At least five assumptions underlie the use of this text in support of segregation. They are as follows: (1) that God pronounced the curse, (2) that the curse be biologically transferable, (3) that Ham be the original victim of the curse, (4) that the children of the original victim of the curse be slaves, (5) that the original victim of the curse be a member of the Negroid race.

But are these valid assumptions? Can they be justified by appeal to the scriptures?

One of the above-quoted verses indicates the absence of any basis whatever for the first assumption. The deliverer of the curse is not God but Noah. And Noah pronounces it some time, it seems, before his return to complete sobriety. This passage raises at least two disturbing questions for Christian segregationists. Is it not a rather precarious business to hold God responsible for the curse of any man? Should we not be even more reluctant to hold God responsible for the curse of a drunken man?

We come now to the question underlying the second assumption. Does the Bible sanction the condemnation of one generation of men for the offense of another? The biblical answer to this question can be either Yes or No. It all depends on which biblical proverb you accept as more nearly expressive of the mind of God. If you choose, you can answer with Ezekiel's contemporaries that "the fathers have eaten sour grapes, and the children's teeth are set on edge" (18:2)—but not without denying Ezekiel's claim to be God's spokesman. For Ezekiel declares in the Lord's name: "The son shall not bear the iniquity of the father, neither shall the father bear the iniquity of the son: the righteousness of the righteous shall be upon him, and the wickedness of the wicked shall be upon him." (18:20.) Of course, if somebody objects to this interpretation of one text in the light of another, so much the better—for the text of Noah's curse, unlike so many of the curses which appear in the Bible, makes no mention whatever of the victim's children; neither of his children's children; nor of the children of generations yet unborn.

This brings us to the third assumption of this argument, and, simultaneously, to an extraordinarily incredible phenomenon about the use of this story as a ground for the perpetuation of Noah's curse of Ham on his children's children to the hundredth generation. This is the absence of Ham's name from the text of the verse in which Noah invokes the curse. That is to say, taking the text as it stands, the curse falls not on Ham, but on Canaan, one of Ham's four children. In other words, even conceding the possibility of the perpetuation of the disastrous effects of such a curse through all human history, three fourths of Ham's descendants have no reason to regard themselves as the heirs of Canaan's curse.

We come now to the question underlying the fourth assumption governing the use of this curse as a biblical anticipation of segregation: What about its effects? Or to put it more sharply, Did Canaan become Shem and Japheth's "servant of servants"? Quite the contrary; Canaan's descendants dominated the whole land of Palestine until long after the death of Moses, and Jerusalem, which took its name from Canaan's son Jebus, remained in Canaanite hands until David led Israel in its capture. According to the people who treat Gen. 1–11 as sober history, this happened about seventeen centuries after the invocation of Noah's curse on Canaan! Moreover, the alleged inferiority of Ham's immediate descendants falls in the same category as their alleged servitude. Indeed, granted the historicity of the geographical distribution of this passage, the only possible conclusion would be just the reverse of this notion.

For the last 3000 years the world has been mainly indebted for its advancement to the Shemitic and Indo-European races; but it was otherwise in the first ages. Egypt and Babylon, Mizraim and Nimrod —both descendants of Ham—led the way and acted as pioneers of mankind in the various fields of art, literature, and science. [Italics mine.] Alphabetic writing, astronomy, history, . . . agriculture, textile industry—seem, all of them, to have had their origin in one or the other of these two countries.[9]

Considering the length of time (seventeen centuries!) it took this curse to begin to take effect, it must have been either the pronouncement of a man who misread the mind of God, or of a deity incapable of making good on his pronouncement. Forced to choose between these alternatives, who of us would take the latter?

Now for a look at the designation of the Canaanites as Negroes. According to Josephus' *Antiquities of the Jews,* "Canaan, the fourth son of Ham, inhabited the country now called Judaea, and named it after himself, Canaan." [10] So our question becomes this: Were the pre-Israelite inhabitants of Palestine Negroid in type? W. F. Albright, generally recognized as the leading biblical archaeologist of our day, answers this question with an unequivocal and emphatic negative. As a matter of fact, according to this distinguished authority, all known ancient races in the region of the Old Testament world "belonged to the so-called 'white' or 'Caucasian' race, with the exception of the Cushites [Ethiopians] who were strongly Negroid in type." [11]

Before bidding farewell to this passage, let us briefly review the steps we have to take in order to derive from it biblical support for segregation. We must make God responsible for a curse the Bible puts in the mouth of Noah. We must inflict the effects of this curse on people a hundred or more generations removed from its original victim. We must substitute Ham for Canaan as the original victim of the curse. We must rewrite the history of of antiquity in such a way as to turn masters into

26

slaves and slaves into masters. And by the same token, Negroes into Caucasians and Caucasians into Negroes!

The Confusion at Babel

The biblical account of the confusion of tongues at Babel (Gen. 11:1-9) marks another frequently quoted text in the brief against integration. "This was an act of special Divine Providence," asserts one writer, "to frustrate the mistaken efforts of godless men to assure the permanent integration of the peoples of the earth." [12] And why did God perform it? Because it was "the most effective means of preserving the separate existence of the several racial groups." [13]

Basic to this argument are these four assumptions: (1) that God inflicted the confusion of tongues on men as a penalty for their attempt at racial integration, (2) that the existence of linguistic differences denotes progress among men, (3) that linguistic differences and racial differences are coextensive, (4) that the division of men after the fall be along racial lines.

The text of Gen. 11 offers small comfort indeed to those who turn to it in search of the validation of this first assumption. The Lord does not punish mankind at Babel for their attempted integration of the human race. He punishes them for their attempted integration of God and men.

Neither does the text support the second assumption. God does not afflict men with multiple languages until after they sin. He confuses the tongues of men as a penalty for their erection of a Babylonian skyscraper. Apparently we would still be living in a one-language world if the builders of the tower of Babel had not explored the upper atmosphere.

The third assumption, without which the whole argument falls of its own weight, can be answered in few words. Here we

27

have only to consider American racial and linguistic differences. Whereas the city of New York has integrated all three major races despite the use of multiple tongues, numerous mill towns of the country have segregated the Negroes and whites despite the use of a common tongue. Considering this fact, do not those of us who hail "the confusion of tongues" as "an act of special Divine Providence" to preserve racial segregation come dangerously close to blasphemy? Who are we to say that God—whom some of us hail as "the Original Segregationist"—had he been so vitally interested in segregation, could have offered no better plan of segregation than one that does not segregate?

The text offers no stronger support for the fourth of the above assumptions than it does for the first three. The people involved in the division of mankind which follows hard on the heels of the destruction of the tower of Babel, from first to last, are all alike the descendants of Shem. This may be taken as additional evidence, not only of the irrelevance of this text to the issue of race, but also of its exclusive preoccupation, as A. S. Peake notes, with this question: *"Why is it that though the races of mankind have sprung from a common ancestry they speak so many different languages?"* [14]

CHAPTER II

The Demands for Racial Purity

WE SHALL BE DEALING IN THIS CHAPTER WITH THE ISSUE TO WHICH many segregationists attribute their oposition to integration. They favor segregation, they say, because we cannot have the integration of the races without contributing to the amalgamation of the races. Despite the many interesting questions raised by this contention, we shall be concerned only with the claim to biblical support for opposition to mixed marriages. This calls for the consideration of two questions: Does the Bible prohibit mixed marriages? or to put it positively, Does the Bible attach special virtue to racial purity?

The Ban on Mixtures

In no instance do segregationists more clearly betray the difficulty of finding biblical support for their cause than in their use of the Levitical prohibition of mixtures. The verse in question reads as follows: "Thou shalt not let thy cattle gender with a diverse kind: thou shalt not sow thy field with mingled seed: neither shall a garment mingled of linen and woollen come upon thee" (Lev. 19:19). Gillespie has written in defense of his use of this verse in support of segregation: "If such intermixture in the lower orders of animal and plant life were unseemly and contrary to the Divine purpose, the same principle would apply with even greater force with respect to human relations." [1]

This particular prohibition has a threefold reference. It proscribes the breeding of different kinds of cattle, the sowing of different kinds of seed in a field, and the use of different fabrics

29

in a garment. Before stretching the ban on the intermixture of cattle to include human beings, should we not first pause to ask whether this reference ever applied to the lower animals? If so, apparently neither David nor Ahab knew of any such legislation. At any rate, the Bible refers—and without either explanation or apology—to the presence of mules at the courts of both.[2] Nor has Christianity introduced any significant change in the status of these hybrids. Churches have nowhere closed their parishes to mules, and mules everywhere have taken advantage of this attitude toward hybrids. The rapid advances in mechanization notwithstanding, they still roam the countryside of America as beasts of burden. And not only do they do so without respect for regional or racial differences, but they do so without either civil or ecclesiastical handicap.

The prohibition against the use of a mixture of seeds in a field has been equally ineffective. Indeed, if this prohibition were suddenly to be enforced, almost every lawn in the country worth a second look would have to undergo an emergency operation at the hands of some horticultural surgeon.

The third prohibition has not fared any better. A merchant with little enough sense to stock 100 per cent wool suits with 100 per cent wool linings would soon go 100 per cent bankrupt. In short, if such intermixtures in the lower orders of plant and animal life be "unseemly and contrary to the Divine purpose," then we must be just about the most unseemly and disobedient generations with which God has yet had to deal.

But since Gillespie cites this passage in support of racial segregation, obviously he construes this legislation as a ban on all mixtures of color in animals, plants, and fabrics. But he does not say so. Not once does he suggest the exclusion of the owners of Holstein heifers or Dominique chickens from membership in societies for the preservation of segregation. Neither does he propose the excommunication of all fruitgrowers who haul Grimes Golden and Virginia Beauty apples from the same orchard. Nor does he imply a ban on all members of women's auxiliaries whose officers wear pheasant feathers in their hats. Yet he cites this passage as evidence of God's demand for the segregation of human beings on the basis of color!

Now for a summary of the argument for racial segregation from this text: Though we no longer have to avoid the mixtures expressly condemned in this passage, we must treat it as the biblical warrant for avoidance of a mixture it does not even mention. We do not have to segregate cattle, seeds, and fabrics of different colors—despite the Levitical prohibition of any intermixture of cattle, seeds, or fabrics—but we must segregate human beings of different colors, though the text never mentions human beings.

If segregationists really consider the race question a problem in human relations, it is not at all surprising to see them turn to the nineteenth chapter of Leviticus in search of light on it. But the use they make of it is surprising—not only because of the verse they do consider, but even more because of the verses they completely ignore. You see, if they were to explore all the verses of this chapter, they would not have to draw their conclusions about human relations on the basis of a biblical statement about cattle. They would discover some quite pointed suggestions which deal specifically and exclusively with human relations. For example, Jesus thought so well of the verse which immediately precedes Lev. 19:19 that he used it as the second half of his summary of the Great Commandment. This verse ends with the words: ". . . thou shalt love thy neighbour as thyself: I am the Lord." Whereas Jesus ignored the nineteenth verse and quoted the eighteenth, the segregationists ignore the

31

eighteenth and quote the nineteenth. Even more surprising is their disregard of the thirty-fourth and thirty-fifth verses of ch. 19, for these verses discuss the proper treatment by Israelites of non-Israelites—and without the faintest suggestion of any distinction between Caucasian strangers and Negroid strangers. "And if a stranger sojourn with thee in your land, ye shall not vex him. But the stranger that dwelleth with you shall be unto you as one born among you, and thou shalt love him as thyself; for ye were strangers in the land of Egypt.

The Plea for Purity

Many segregationists claim the Bible as the source of their insistence that racial purity is a requirement of Almighty God. Apparently aware of the failure of the Bible to include any such requirement as a sort of eleventh commandment, they justify their derivation of this principle from the Bible in a variety of ways. A few trace the disasters of certain biblical characters to their foreign wives; thus, they defend their contention that nothing good can come of a mixed marriage. Some cite the racial purity of the Jews as proof of history's reservation of her choisest plums for people of a pure race. Others stress the hopeless inferiority of the products of mixed marriages. But they have not attempted a thorough study of the biblical evidence on this question. And understandably so too, for if they had, they would have been forced to concede the possibility of finding ample biblical documentation for at least three arguments in conflict with their position.

First of all, they would have found innumerable instances of intermarriage between Hebrews and non-Hebrews. These are found where one would least expect to find the record of such occurrences—in the very same books which call for the separation of the Hebrews. Genesis contains the record of at least five inter-marriages of this sort (16:3; 38:2; 41:50); Exodus at least one (2:21) and possibly a host of others (12:38); Leviticus one (24:10); Numbers one (12:1) and probably many others (see 11:4; cf. 31:9, 18); and Deuteronomy, while it records no specific instance of such marriage, makes legal provision for the marriage of Israelite men to the women of conquered peoples (21:10-13). Many additional examples of the intermixture of Israelites with non-Israelites could be adduced from other Old Testament books.

Too, if they had prepared a list of all the parties to and products of mixed marriages, doubtless they would have been greatly surprised at some of the names on it. If complete, such a list would include the names of Abraham, Joseph, Moses, David, Solomon, and Jesus of Nazareth, to mention only a few of the outstanding characters of the Bible. What better evidence could we have of the failure of the Bible to attach an indelible stigma to mixed marriages? [3]

Moreover, if they had traced the family trees of those figures against the Genesis table of nations, they would have found traces of Hamitic connections in the ancestry of the star performers in the drama of biblical religion. Not only do Abraham, Joseph, and Solomon take unto themselves wives from peoples descended from Ham, but so also does Moses (Num. 12:1). And when Aaron and Miriam condemn him for this marriage, according to the twelfth chapter of the book of Numbers, the Lord sides with Moses against his brother and sister, saying unto them in 12:7-8:

My servant Moses . . . is faithful in all mine house. With him will I speak mouth to mouth, . . . and not in dark speeches; and the similitude of the Lord shall he behold: wherefore then were ye not afraid to speak against my servant Moses.

Then, according to the Gospel of Matthew, the genealogy of Jesus of Nazareth included Rachab, a woman of the Canaanites (see Josh. 2:1 ff.), a people begotten by Canaan (Gen. 10: 18-19), one of the four sons of Ham (Gen. 6:10)—the one, in fact, on whom the famous curse fell!

We have yet to consider the precedent to which segregationists most often point in defense of their claim to biblical support. That is the oft-recurring biblical demand for a pure Israel. Since Israel's prophets and priests demanded the separation of peoples, why should we not demand the separation of races? What's the difference, they ask, between our demand for a pure race and their demand for a pure Israel? For obvious reasons, they would not ask such a question if they did not feel free to employ the biblical demand for a pure Israel in support of their plea for segregation. But are they right in this assumption? Is the parallel sufficiently close to justify it?

This question calls for a detailed examination of the background of the biblical demand for a pure Israel. This insistence reaches a peak at two points in Israelite history, once during the period between the Exodus and the Exile, and again during the postexilic period of Nehemiah and Ezra. Is there any special reason why such a demand should have arisen during these periods?

During the first period, and almost without exception, Israel's great prophets condemn association with the Canaanites, the pre-Israelite inhabitants of Palestine. They do so for two principal reasons. One is the difference between Israelite and Canaanite culture. The prophets fear, and for good reason, the capitulation of their nomadic mode of life to the agricultural and commercial civilization of the Canaanites. The other is the difference between Israelite and Canaanite religion. The prophets abhor the very thought of the triumph of Baalism, the Canaanite religion, over Yahwism, the religion of Israel. Why?

Not as the casual reader would be inclined to think, because of the miserable bigotry which refuses to recognize the spirit of God in any save one's own group, but because of the nature of Baalism itself. The prophets object to Baalism because of the evils which attend the worship of the gods of Canaan.[4] Hand in hand with this worship go such degrading practices as child sacrifice and female prostitution. Besides, fellowship with the gods does not mark the chief end of such worship. It has as its primary aim the enlistment of divine aid in quest of good crops —it's almost a case of consider your need and choose your god. Even its services of worship betray the crassly materialistic flavor of Canaanite religion. They major in wine, women, and song. They sanction both male and female prostitution; indeed, they glamorize sex to a degree only Paris and Hollywood have since been able to rival.

These considerations demonstrate the absurdity of the attempt to enlist the prophet's plea for Israelite separation from the Canaanites in support of the current clamor for the separation of the whites of America from the Negroes of America. Any such effort is doomed to failure from the outset, and for two rather obvious reasons. One is the absence of any real parallel between ancient Israelite and modern American culture, white or Negro. The prophets would be even more strongly opposed to our culture than they were to that of the Canaanites, and for the same identical reason: our culture is more agricultural and commercial than pastoral or nomadic. The other reason is the absence of

35

any comparable difference in religion. American Negroes and American whites, unlike the Israelites and Canaanites, share "one Lord, one faith, one baptism" (Eph. 4:5) and, as often as not, hold membership in the same denomination, claim a common history, read from the same liturgy, sing from the same hymnal, preach the same gospel, extol the same moral principles, and labor for the same goals.

A similar crisis gave birth to the separatist movement, spearheaded by Nehemiah and Ezra, during the postexilic period, Within a quarter of a century after the return from Babylon, returnees and natives joined hands in the restoration of the Jerusalem temple. This feat accomplished, the Jews began to breathe easily for a change, anticipating the break of fortune in their favor. But it did not come. Instead, their lot soon took a decided turn for the worse. The inhabitants of Jerusalem found the going especially rough. As if natural calamities had not done them enough damage, the temptation to spiritual defection arose from another source. Foreigners in the city were working both publicly and privately for the corruption of Jewish faith and worship. And with considerable success too! Consequently, when Nehemiah, a Jew who had won favor at the Persian court, heard the grim news, he took immediate and decisive action. He got himself appointed governor of Judea. After arriving in Palestine, he lost no time in pressing for a careful study of the situation—nor in taking action. His preliminary study convinced him that the restoration of the city walls of Jerusalem would do much to check the religious decline. So he acted accordingly. He launched a building program to this end, and it was brought to an early and successful climax. At least Nehemiah must have thought it successful, for he celebrated its completion with a return to Persia.

His next visit to Judea thoroughly disillusioned him. He found a worse situation than greeted him on his first visit. Priests were exploiting public piety for private gain. They were even permitting the desecration of the temple by foreigners. Worst of all, vast numbers of Jews had abandoned sabbath observance.

This time, determined to get at the root of the trouble, Nehemiah made a much more careful analysis of the situation. Mixed marriages, he finally concluded, constituted the basic problem. As a result of these marriages, wholesale conversion had been taking place, but in the wrong direction. Instead of Jewish husbands and wives winning their mates to Judaism, just the opposite had been happening. And at such a dizzy pace Nehemiah feared for the future of Judaism. Convinced of the need for revolutionary action, he took it. He exacted an oath from Jewish parents that they would never grant permission for the marriage of their children to non-Jews. (Neh. 13:23-31.)

But even this action failed of its purpose. When Ezra, another prominent Jew of the Diaspora, arrived in Palestine, he found a horrifying situation. Religious indifference had become the rule rather than the exception. Why? Like Nehemiah, he laid the blame at the door of foreign mates. Apparently intermarriage between Jews and non-Jews had taken place, Nehemiah's plea to the contrary notwithstanding. Convinced of the failure of this attempt to deal with the problem, Ezra felt the need for a really drastic solution,[5] which he proposed too, and without delay. He ordered the immediate dissolution of all marriages between Jews and non-Jews. (Ezra 10:10-11.) Following a long list of names, the book of Ezra ends with this note: "All these had married foreign women, and they put them away with their children" (R.S.V.).

At least four difficulties obstruct the use by Christians of

Ezra's demand as a biblical precedent for the practice of segregation. For one thing, Ezra's demands are rooted in a concern for religious and not racial purity. He demands the divorce of non-Jewish mates, not because they pose a threat to the purity of Jewish blood, but because they are corrupting Jewish religion. This being the case, just what, from Ezra's viewpoint, would a pure and undefiled religion require of man?

It would require nothing less than the strict observance of the law. While scholars cannot agree as to the identity of the law for whose observance Ezra pleaded, this detail does not really affect the problem at hand. For even if we take the shorter version as the handbook of Ezra's religion, we find ourselves face to face with a whole host of religious duties, rites, and festivals which are as foreign to modern Christians as the Jews' non-Jewish mates were objectionable to Ezra. Indeed, from the very beginning we Christians have asserted our freedom from the religious system of Ezra.[6]

This being the case, just how can we Christians cite Ezra in support of a separatist doctrine without putting ourselves in an anomalous position? Since we do not even attempt the practice of the religion which constituted the sole reason for Ezra's plea for the separation of Jews from non-Jews, how can we possibly rationalize our use of that plea as a biblical sanction for the separation of one group of Gentiles from another group of Gentiles?

In the second place, the Bible itself contains two vigorous protests of Ezra's decree against the intermarriage of Jews and non-Jews. The first of these, the book of Ruth, relates the story of the marriage of a Moabite widow to Boaz. Obed, an offspring of this union, begets Jesse, the father of David.

Most scholars find in this story a subtle, yet powerful, criticism of the exclusivism of Ezra and Nehemiah. Of course, to appreciate the story fully, we have to recall the place of David in Israelite thought and affection. Because he had been the king of the most glorious and glamorous period of Israel's past, Jews could scarcely envision a return of Israelite glory without the return of a son of David. It is as though the author were asking his contemporaries, nurtured in the viewpoint of Ezra, the ironical question: "If David had foreign blood in him, why should you be passing laws and issuing decrees to keep it out of your children?"

The book of Jonah, another brilliant though brief work, voices a similar plea. It resembles Ruth in style, outlook, and aim. Jonah, who detests all foreigners, especially Assyrians, receives a call from God to go to Assyria and preach there a message of repentance. The unwilling Jonah does everything short of committing suicide in his effort to escape this unpleasant assignment. But finally, thanks to a helpful fish and despite the reluctant prophet, God employs Jonah as the mouthpiece of his call of the Assyrians to repentance. All the Assyrians, including the women and the cattle, cover themselves with sackcloth in response to the call of God. Here the author's implied question becomes even more ironical than that of Ruth: "If God does not hold himself aloof from foreigners, what right do you have to hold yourselves aloof from them?"

Third, the perspective of the Christian faith more closely resembles that of Ruth and Jonah than that of Ezra and Nehemiah. For example, just why does the author of Ruth make a Moabitess the heroine of his story? For the same reason Jesus makes a Samaritan the hero of his famous parable. He cites this instance of Jewry's indebtedness to a hated people, in the hope of saving Judaism from a stultifying arrogance. And why does the author of Jonah record his striking example of successful evangelism on Assyrian soil? To protest the attempt of narrow Jews to reduce the heart of God to the size of theirs. More important still, he is asserting God's attachment of greater significance to other matters than Jewish descent—such matters, for example, as justice, mercy, love, humility, generosity. Indeed, this author's view of religion comes within a hair's breadth of that of Jesus, expressed so vividly in the words of the First Gospel: "For whosoever shall do the will of my Father which is in heaven, the same is my brother, and sister, and mother" (Matt. 12:50).

Finally, before treating Ezra 10:10 as a proof text for segregation, Christians ought to take another look at the genealogies of Jesus in the Gospels of Matthew and Luke. These genealogies reveal just how little respect early Christian writers had for Ezra's demand for a pure stock. Since we could employ these texts as proof of Jesus' inability to meet Ezra's requirements for consideration as a member of the chosen people, how can we justify the imposition of such requirements on Jesus' followers?

Now for a summary of the biblical defenses of a separatist doctrine. Always such demands stem from a concern for the purity of religion rather than race. But these demands do not always spotlight the same religious emphases. One group of them emphasizes cultic and ceremonial factors as well as moral and spiritual considerations. The other emphasizes moral and spiritual factors to the virtual exclusion of cultic and ceremonial factors. Certainly there can be no question as to which of these traditions framed the background of the Christian movement. It was the latter and not the former.

CHAPTER III

The Scope of Christian Love

CHRISTIAN THINKERS DIVIDE THEMSELVES INTO NUMEROUS GROUPS by their answers to almost every question save one. The question concerns the place of love in Christian faith. Christian theologians of all varieties see love as the heart and soul of the gospel. But here the agreement ends. They cannot agree as to what adjectives, whether "heedless" or "mutual," should be used to describe it. Nor can they agree as to the proper boundaries for the exercise of such love.

Considering the general diversity of opinion concerning the definition and application of Christian love, it is not surprising that Christian segregationists should join the issue. We have no reason to be shocked by their proposal of a new interpretation of the meaning of Christian love, nor by their attempt to justify the denial of such love in certain specific circumstances to certain particular people or institutions.

The Definition

S. E. Rogers has advanced the most disconcerting biblical argument for segregation. *He grounds his support of segregation in Christian love.*[1] In an address before the Manning, South Carolina, Lions Club, he excoriated modern ministers for their gross negligence and inexcusable ignorance.[2] He said they had to be guilty of one or the other, or both, or they would have called attention to the New Testament's definition of Christian love in such terms as to justify the practice of segregation. Now how does the New Testament effect this achievement? Through a thoroughly consistent distinction, Rogers says, in its use of the two Greek words for love which he transliterates as *agapao* and *fileo*.

Now for a look at Roger's formulation of his case:

Agapao denotes the love of reason, of esteem, of respect. *Fileo* denotes the love of feeling, of affection. Throughout the New Testament the word that is used to express God's love to man, man's love to God, and the love of Christians for each other is *agapao*—respect, esteem. Jesus brought out the distinction when, speaking of his relationship to God in John 5:20, he said, "For the Father loves (*fileo*) the Son"; but when he speaks of man's love for Christ (John 8:42) he says, "If God were your father, ye would love (*agapao*) me."

Christian love, then, is the love of reason, of respect, of esteem, and such love is completely compatible with a segregated society. It is far different from the love of feeling and affection upon which an integrated society would be based, and from which relationships calling for such love would naturally flow.

I can *agapao* the Negro, I can respect him. He can merit my esteem. We can be one in Jesus Christ in our mutual respect and esteem for Christ and for each other. However, I cannot *fileo* him, nor do I want him to *fileo* me; nor do I want the relationship existing between him and me that filial love implies; and neither Christ nor Christianity requires such love.[3]

Before evaluating this argument, let us remind ourselves again of its novelty. We do not consider it because of its widespread use—seldom has anyone other than Rogers even mentioned it. It is really much too sophisticated to capture the popular mind. This being the case, why should we even pause to consider it?

Because practically all the Christian advocates of segregation, though few of them ever articulate it, take it for granted.

Two of Roger's observations lie beyond dispute. The New Testament does employ two Greek words for love, *agapao* and *phileo*. Moveover, it is probably true that *agapao* connotes little of the warmth of *phileo*.[4] But here the validity of Roger's argument begins to break down.

It is not really true, as Rogers contends, that the Greek New Testament restricts itself to some form of *agapao* "to express God's love to man, man's love to God, and the love of Christians for each other." The New Testament can, and indeed does, employ some form of the verb *phileo* to express each of these various loves. Jesus employs a form of *phileo* to express God's love for man, when he says in John 16:27 (R.S.V.): "For the Father himself loves [*philei*] you." When Paul alerts the Christians in Corinth to the danger of the absence of love for Christ, he writes: "If any man love [*philei*] not the Lord Jesus Christ, let him be accursed" (I Cor. 16:22). And *phileo* may also be used to express the love of one man for another (see Matt. 10:37).

But the really crucial defect of Roger's contention has yet to be indicated. Despite the above exceptions to Rogers' generalization concerning the preference in the Greek New Testament for *agapao* or some form of it, his generalization concerning the use of this word in the New Testament still holds. Indeed, the word for love in the New Testament is so often some form of *agapao* that a few scholars call it the distinctively Christian word for love. But not, as Rogers suggests, because it allows for discrimination among the recipients of such love. Rather, as the great Swedish theologian Anders Nygren insists, the New Testament preference for some form of *agapao* to express the meaning of Christian love has just the opposite explanation. It is not because of the inability of *agapao* to communicate deep feeling. It stems rather from *agapao's* utter disregard of every external condition, whether righteousness, religion, or race, which might qualify its strength.[5]

We look in vain for an explanation of God's love in the character of the man who is the object of His love. . . . God's love is altogether *spontaneous*. It does not look for anything in man that could be adduced as motivation for it. . . . When it is said that God loves man, this is not a judgment on what man is like, but on what God is like.[6]

Now let us summarize Roger's argument and its basic error. He is quite right in calling attention to the New Testament's preference for some form of *agapao* over *phileo* to express the idea of love. But he is utterly wrong in his argument that the latter type of love is of a more demanding sort. As we have already pointed out, these two terms do not necessarily denote two different types of love; either may be, and in the New Testament is, used to describe all the various relationships of the religious life: God to man, man to God, and man to man. The New Testament aversion for *phileo*, insofar as such an aversion characterizes the New Testament, may be traced to the popular tendency to think of love (*phileo*) as a reciprocal relationship, rooted in a common attraction and sustained by mutual interests. Therefore, when the New Testament adopts *agapao* rather than *phileo* as its standard word for love, it reminds us of this basic fact about the nature of true Christian love: that it tells us nothing at all about our neighbor.[7] Nothing about the size of his fortune, nothing of the state of his soul—nothing of the color of his skin. It tells us only this one fact: that he is beloved of God. And this, not because the neighbor is lovable,

44

but because *God's love is indeed blind love*—value blind, creed blind, and, yes, color blind too.

The Application

The next biblical argument for segregation raises the whole issue of the Christian's obligation to the state. Here texts are seldom quoted. As a rule, biblical support for a hostile attitude to the state is just assumed. For example, the author of a notably forthright invitation to defy the Supreme Court decision against segregation does not cite any particular scriptural passage in support of his position. Yet the wording of his statement clearly reflects the assumption of a biblical basis for his view. Here are excerpts from his statement:

Who are we, poor, mortal beings, to question the great wisdom of the Divinity in separating the races [although he does not cite any biblical reference, apparently he has in mind Gen. 9:18-29] into three great species of man? Shall we defy all the laws of nature and God and integrate? . . .

We do not have to bow abjectly to this unconstitutional judicial legislation by a supreme court that is no longer supreme in the minds of the people.[8]

These words seem to suggest defiance of the state out of respect for God's requirement of segregation as set forth in the Bible. If so, then this argument presupposes the biblical sanction of two things: (1) the geographical division of the races, (2) the resistance of any attempt by the state to force integration. We have already analyzed the biblical basis of this first assumption. So we may limit ourselves here to an examination of the New Testament view (we shall look at the Old Testament view of the state in Part II) of the scope of the authority of the state in such matters. Indeed, the question may be even more narrowly circumscribed. Under what circumstances, if any, does the New Testament sanction defiance of the state? Can we ground the plea for resistance to the state's (in this case, of course, the national state) implementation of the Supreme Court's ban on segregation in the New Testament teaching on the Christian's relation to the state? Or since all of us, regardless of our feeling about segregation, must face the question of our responsibility to the state on this issue, what is the New Testament view of the state?

Most scholars deny the existence of anything approximating a clear and consistent solution to the problem of the relationship between church and state in the New Testament. At the same time, however, they find slight justification in its writings for resistance to the state.[9] Millar Burrows, in the following statement, reflects the majority opinion of contemporary biblical scholars on the question of the Christian attitude to the state in the New Testament:

Jesus is concerned with a man's relation to God, not with his relation to the Roman government. In his own ministry, he endeavors to avoid political complications. It seems ironical that he was put to death as a revolutionist. . . . Paul enjoyed . . . the protection of the Roman authorities against his Jewish opponents; naturally therefore he commanded submission. . . . A similar attitude is expressed in I Peter 2:13-17. . . . A new attitude appears in Revelation: Rome is the great harlot, drunk with the blood of the saints and martyrs; the empire is the beast, incarnate especially in the person of Nero. Yet the book is no call to revolt; it teaches steadfast but passive resistance. Faithfulness and endurance in persecution are urged also in Hebrews and in I Peter.[10]

46

If this be the correct interpretation of the matter, then the New Testament attitude to the authority of the civil state can be defined quite simply as that of unqualified obedience. That is, except when it demands the elevation of the state or its head above God. When Caesar thus invades the sphere of God, the Christian has the duty of resistance to the death. But—and this is important—not against the state's right to issue such a decree. What he must resist is the state's power to compel personal conformity to its blasphemous demand. Hence such resistance can scarcely be anything more than a martyr's testimony to the futility of Rome's effort to usurp the powers or place of God.

Now let us attempt the determination of the duty of the Christian segregationist in the light of this principle. Since Christian love precludes recourse to violence, he can hardly ground the right to sedition in the teaching of the New Testament. By no means can he claim the New Testament as an excuse for all-out resistance to the state because of the degradation of "the supreme court" in the popular mind. All he can offer in resistance, according to this view, is his own nonconformity and personal witness.

However, before leaving this matter, we should consider the implications of a recent challenge to the traditional interpretation of the New Testament attitude to the state for the problem at hand. Especially since its author, Oscar Cullmann, enjoys an international reputation as a New Testament scholar. If the segregationists could claim only his sanction of their use of the New Testament in defense of open resistance to the state's demand for integration, they would enjoy good, even if somewhat isolated, support.

Cullmann argues, and with considerable cogency, for the New Testament's assumption toward the earthly state of "an attitude based on principle—and yet not in such a way that the State as such would be renounced a priori." [11] Nor does the New Testament expectation of the end become an occasion for indifference to the state. On the contrary, it becomes the source of some quite definite suggestions for dealing with the state. And these are, Cullmann insists, whether you look to the teaching of Jesus, Paul, or the Revelation, as follows:

The Church's task with regard to the State, which is posed for all time, is thus clear. First, it must loyally give the State everything necessary to its existence. It has to oppose anarchy . . . within its own ranks. Second, it has to fulfil the office of watchman over the State. That means: it must remain . . . critical toward every State and be ready to warn it against transgression of its legitimate limits. Third, it must deny to the State which exceeds its limits whatever such a State demands . . . ; and in its preaching the Church must courageously describe this excess as opposition to God.[12]

Granted this solution to the problem of the relationship between church and state, Christians have only one question to ask about the decision outlawing segregation in the public schools. They have only to ask whether the Supreme Court exceeded its limits in its desegregation order. If Cullmann is right in suggesting that such excess cannot be identified with anything less than the state's demand for the elevation of itself to divine status,[13] the Supreme Court quite clearly did not exceed its powers. But even before we come to this point in Cullmann's argument, he raises other hurdles for the segregationists. Can American Christians give to our particular national state "everything necessary to its existence" and oppose desegre-

48

gation? Many people would answer this question in the negative, so convinced are they that the practice of segregation jeopardizes our very existence as a national state. For example, according to one contemporary authority in Christian ethics:

Unless America can rather quickly make her racial practices express good conscience before the conscience of the world, she is not likely to retain the leadership so largely entrusted to her now, or even to retain her own self-respect.[14]

And even if one could oppose the national government for this judicial action without jeopardizing its existence, one would still have to determine the nature of his resistance. Could he resort to violence, or would he have to remain content merely to preach against "this excess as opposition to God"? While Cullmann does not expressly answer this question, is it not significant that he nowhere mentions his discovery in the New Testament of any justification whatever of the former alternative? Had he done so, a still further question would remain to be answered. Could the church take this step without precipitating an outbreak of anarchy, without as well as within its ranks?

The New Testament betrays still another weakness in the attempt of the segregationists to turn its view of the state into a weapon against the Supreme Court. Or it does if the author of the statement on page 45 seriously intended one of the implications of his remarks—that is, the one conveyed by his observation that we do not have to abide by the Supreme Court's decision because it is "no longer supreme in the minds of the people." Is he not implying here that we ought to be able to object to the decisions of any state of which we do not approve? If so, is he not overlooking the fact that the Christian community of Paul's time lived under the rule of a government

49

in the hands of foreigners? And that, despite the widespread resentment occasioned by this fact, practically all the writers of the New Testament counsel obedience to the state? Then, too, is he not also ignoring the fact that the New Testament nowhere suggests that we are free to accept or reject at will the decisions of a properly constituted agency of the state?

Summary

Whether the segregationist adopts the traditional or Cullmann's theory of the New Testament view of the Christian's relation to the state, it makes no practical difference. The New Testament view of the state provides no basis, in either case, for his criticism of the Supreme Court for its antisegregation decision. Neither does it furnish him with an excuse for defiance of the state in its efforts to implement this decision. Nor does it supply him with a biblical sanction for the denial of Christian love, whether *agapao* or *phileo*, to certain fellow citizens—even if some of his neighbors do treat them as second-class citizens.

PART II

Are There Biblical Precedents for Segregation?

Introduction

MANY SEGREGATIONISTS FRANKLY CONCEDE THE FAILURE OF THE Bible to treat race explicitly and categorically as a basis for the separation of peoples. But they contend for the right to treat all biblical sanctions of the principle of separatism as precedents for the practice of racial segregation.

The evaluation of this claim calls for consideration of at least the following questions: Does the Bible really sanction the practice of separatism? If so, can such instances of the support of the practice of separatism be construed as an unqualified endorsement of separatism as a general principle? That is to say, do the authors of such sanctions conceive them as permanent solutions to universal problems for all time? Or do they view them merely as temporary solutions to local problems for a limited time? These are the questions with which we shall be concerned in the next three chapters.

CHAPTER IV

The Doctrine
of a Limited Brotherhood

JAMES L. FOWLE, PASTOR OF THE FIRST PRESBYTERIAN CHURCH OF Chattanooga, Tennessee, ignited a battle royal among the ministers of that city with his criticism of a campaign by the Junior Chamber of Commerce to secure blood-donor pledges on the basis of the brotherhood of man. For several days thereafter, despite the continuation of hostilities in Korea, the citizens of Chattanooga took an uncommon interest in the progress of this theological fracas. This caused much embarrassment to the American Red Cross, the Department of Defense, and the National Conference of Christians and Jews, as well as the Junior Chamber of Commerce, since all these organizations had sought such pledges through the use of a card containing the reminder, "As God is the Father of all men, so all men are brothers." [1]

Denouncing this statement as a Unitarian creed, Dr. Fowle proceeded to deny a place for it in Trinitarian Christianity. "We in Trinitarian faiths," he declared, "believe only in the brotherhood of men in Christ. We are glad to give our blood for our boys in Korea, but to call these Communists brothers when they are killing our men and would destroy our churches and our American way of life is a position we are not willing to take." [2] Robert Cousar, pastor of the Central Presbyterian Church, joined the battle on the side of Dr. Fowle. "We can only be a brother to one who is a son of our Father, and this link is only possible in Christ," [3] he contended.

Apparently these ministers never paused to consider the fact that their argument called for the denial of blood to all non-Christian Koreans, regardless of their location with reference to the thirty-eighth parallel or their attitude to the Kremlin. And, by the same token, to all non-Christian American soldiers. But these considerations notwithstanding, neither man budged from his apparent stand in favor of rewriting the hymn "In Christ there is no East or West" to read "In Christ there is no East but only West."

Nor did this plea for the introduction of a Christian ghetto end with the cessation of hostilities in Korea. In fact, some of our Christian brethren have not had to go outside our own continental boundaries to find human beings with whom they refuse to claim a family relationship. With the announcement of the now famous Supreme Court decision of May 17, 1954, several hitherto unknown advocates of the doctrine of a limited brotherhood appeared on the scene. They did not employ this argument to keep Christian blood out of Communist countries. They invoked it to justify the practice of racial segregation in a Christian country. They invoked the doctrine of Christian brotherhood in connection with their plea for the resistance by "every Bible believer" of every attempt at integration. For example, E. K. Oldham supported this plea with the flat declaration: "All men are not brothers." [4]

At least three assumptions underlie this defense of segregation from the standpoint of the New Testament view of Christian brotherhood. They are as follows: (1) the exclusive application of the concepts of the fatherhood of God and the brotherhood of man in the New Testament to members of the Christian community, (2) the refusal of association with all persons outside the Christian fellowship, and (3) either the limitation of membership in the household of faith on racial grounds or the segregation of its members along racial lines. Unless these assumptions can be defended in the light of the teaching of the New Testament, then the argument for segregation from the New Testament view of Christian brotherhood must be declared out of bounds.

The first of these assumptions gets emphatic support from Madeline B. Bartlette, an ardent segregationist, who says:

Any Christian who knows his Bible, and has not been fed a "diluted, indoctrinated version," is aware that there is only one Brotherhood of Man taught in the New Testament. This is the spiritual Brotherhood of Born-Again Christians. It has nothing to do with sociological reforms. God is the Creator of all, but He is the Father of only those who have accepted His Son as their Redeemer.[5]

What shall we say of this affirmation? [6] Does the New Testament view of God limit his fatherhood to the action of men? Does rebellion against God terminate the offender's membership in the divine family? Here the question is not whether a flagrantly disobedient creature of God can enjoy an ideal family relationship with the Father, but can he have any sort of family relationship with God? Is God in any sense the Father of the disobedient man—or the disobedient man in any sense the son of God? There are numerous passages we could study in search of the New Testament answer to this question. But we may quite properly, I think, content ourselves with the consideration of only two selections, inasmuch as they are of such decisive importance for the determination of the bearing of the God-man relationship on the question of man's attitude toward his fellows.

56

Let's begin with a look at the familiar parable in Luke 15:11-32. Though the younger son says to his father on his return home, "I am no more worthy to be called thy son," the father says to his servants: "Bring forth the best robe, and put it on him; and put a ring on his hand, and shoes on his feet: and bring hither the fatted calf, and kill it; and let us eat, and be merry: for this my son was dead, and is alive again; he was lost, and is found." The prodigal in the far country, though "dead" and "lost," never ceased to be his father's son. He was more than a dead and lost sinner; he was a dead and lost son. No matter how far he marched off the map of moral respectability, he could not pass beyond the boundaries of his father's love. Though he succeeded in becoming an exile from his father's house, he failed to become an exile from his father's heart or home. The more he felt the inner push of the bent toward self, the stronger he felt the outer pull of the love that would not let him go.

If this story never loses its grip on us, we do not have to look far in search of the reason why. This is the story of our family. The younger son is you or I, and the father is our heavenly Father. Indeed, as George A. Buttrick reminds us in his discussion of the parables of Jesus, this parable of the lost son could better be called "The God of the Lost." [7] For like all the parables of Luke 15, it presupposes this question: "What is God like?" And the answer is crystal clear. He is like "the 'father' in this story." [8]

If we seek a reason for the condemnation of the elder brother, we do not have to go very far in search of that reason. He stands under judgment for his failure to imitate the father of this story. Note the terms of his reference to the restored prodigal. Though his servant and his father both speak to him of "your brother," apparently the elder brother's "family" has no room

57

in it for the repentant wastrel. He speaks of him, in conversation with his father, not as "my brother," but as "this son of yours." But just as the father did not reject the prodigal who left home, so he does not spurn the son who turns prodigal at home. Rather, he turns to him and says, "Son . . ."

What is God like? He is like the father of these two prodigals. He treats his creatures as children whether they deserve it or not. Try as they may to wreck his family, they simply cannot break the yoke of divine fatherhood. Though they take the wings of the morning and join the swine in a far country, the Father's love follows them. And though they make their bed in the pit of self-righteousness, God remains their Father even there.

At an interracial conference in Indianapolis, the pastor of a metropolitan church related the story of the marriage of a young lady of his congregation to a man of whom her parents did not approve. When she proceeded to marry this man in the face of parental advice, they disowned her. Bishop Raines voiced his reaction to this story in these words: "I became my daughter's father the instant she was born. I shall remain her father until I die. Nothing she could ever do could . . . destroy my love for her." [9]

What is God like? He is like the father whose love for his children cannot be destroyed by anything they have done or might do. He is the unconditional lover. If "we love him," let us not forget why. It is "because he first loved us" (I John 4:19).

If the parable of God's love for the younger son illustrates the impossibility of raising a moral barrier to the fatherhood of God, Matt. 5:38-48 does the same for spatial barriers. Just as morality poses no obstacle to God's indiscriminate exercise of his fatherly benevolence, neither does distance. The boundaries

58

of his love coincide with those of his creation (5:45). To be sure, if the verbal hairsplitter chooses, he can object to this interpretation on the ground of the evangelist's failure specifically to employ the terms "Father" and "son" in his description here of the relation of God and man. But two far more important considerations he cannot deny. One is God's bestowal on men—through nature—of a love they do nothing whatever to deserve; "he lavishes sunlight on the niggardly and the generous, and sends rain on the just and the unjust." [10] The other makes the imitation of this same heavenborn love the sole condition of the divine adoption; God adopts as sons only those persons who treat as brothers all on whom he sends the gifts of sunshine and rain.

This passage does not treat membership in the redeemed community as an excuse for the practice of a limited brotherhood. It does just the opposite. It establishes the practice of unconditioned brotherhood as the sole condition of membership in the redeemed community. If you will not have all men for brothers, this passage seems to teach, neither can you have God as Father. As the French theologian Joseph Bonsirven notes in his discussion of "The Duties of God's Children to Their Brethren," the specifically Christian doctrine of brotherly love stems from the biblical insistence on the equality of men in their dependence on God for creation in the divine image. It does not hinge on the inequality of their commitment to his person or the measure of their obedience to his will.[11] This being so, it's hard to see how we can possibly construe the biblical passages which limit the fatherhood of God as justification for the practice of a limited brotherhood. Almost without exception, such passages identify the recognition of mankind as a universal

59

brotherhood as the grounds for admission into the family of which God is Father.

What shall we say now of the assumption of a New Testament ban on association with all persons outside the community of believers? Does the New Testament establish a precedent for the exclusion of nonbelievers from fellowship with "the followers of the way" or the members of "the household of faith"? Though numerous passages of the New Testament have some bearing on this question, we shall limit ourselves to consideration of the companions of our Lord and the attitude of Paul to inter-marriage between believers and unbelievers.

To put it mildly, certain of Jesus' companions shocked some of his contemporaries half out of their wits. As if it were not enough that his friends should come from the wrong side of the ecclesiastical, political, and economic tracks, he associated with the riffraff of society. Then, as if to add insult to injury, after walking the byways in the company of harlots, thieves, and publicans, he singled out just such people as the special target of his ministry, saying: "Those who are well have no need of a physician, but those who are sick; I came not to call the righteous, but sinners" (Mark 2:17 R.S.V.). Rather than giving us an excuse for limiting our association to his followers, the example of Jesus provides us with a challenge for the establish-ment of friendships with people who do not share our faith.

If we can only be a brother to one who has received adoption into the family of God through Christ, as Fowle argued, then surely we could not have an unbeliever for husband or wife. For if Christianity proscribes a close and intimate human rela-tion, such as that of brother and brother, how could it possibly sanction the still more intimate relation of husband and wife

60

between a believer and an unbeliever? Or to put it differently, if it sanctions that of husband and wife, how could it possibly prohibit that of brother and brother?

The Christians at Corinth dumped this problem, along with a host of others, into the lap of the Apostle to the Gentiles. And Paul deals with it in clear and precise terms. Though he seems as little in favor of marriage between believers and unbelievers (II Cor. 6:14) as Ezra of marriage between Jews and Gentiles (Ezra 10:10),[12] he frowns on the use of unbelief as a ground for separation from an unbelieving spouse. "If any brother has a wife who is an unbeliever, and she consents to live with him," he declares, "he should not divorce her. If any woman has a husband who is an unbeliever, and he consents to live with her, she should not divorce him." (I Cor. 7:12-13 R.S.V.) Far from seeing conversion to Christianity as an excuse for the prohibition of any sort of association with non-Christians, Paul advises husbands and wives of unbelievers to continue the most intimate of all human relations.

This brings us to the final question underlying the use of the doctrine of Christian brotherhood in support of segregation. Does the New Testament either limit membership in the Christian community on racial grounds or sanction the segregation of its members along racial lines?

Since the first half of this question is treated elsewhere, we shall pause here only long enough to review the requirements for admission into the Christian community. Does the New Testament ever list membership in a particular race as a prerequisite for participation in the life of the redeemed community?

Despite Jesus' statement concerning the confinement of his

ministry to the house of Israel, in no instance does he distribute the gifts of his ministry on a racial basis. He begins his public ministry with a call for repentance against the background of the nearness of the reign of God (Mark 1:15). While he does not here explicitly preclude additional requirements for admission into the kingdom of God, neither does he mention any other requirements. Nor does he elsewhere in the Gospels. For every single one of the various requirements for participation in the life of the kingdom, as set forth here or there in the teaching of our Lord, can quite accurately be described as one of "the fruits of repentance." [13] Never does he hedge his offer of the kingdom of God with racial or geographical conditions. "The ground of salvation is the undeserved favor of the all-loving Father; it is realized in the individual only by a corresponding acceptance of the proffered gift." [14]

The development of the community of believers into an identifiable and self-conscious ecclesiastical body brought with it, as we have previously noted, a demand for the clarification of the requirements for admission.[15] And unlike so many of the attempts to clarify Christian policy in the heat of controversy, this one produced something more and better than a compromise that settled nothing and pleased nobody. It left churchmen with an admissions policy they could administer without any sort of invidious discrimination throughout the entire world. And these "terms," as Floyd V. Filson correctly observes, "ignore the physical accidents of racial origin, the ritual factors of Mosaic Law, the external conditions in which the gospel finds a person. They focus upon the spiritual and moral aspects, the universal aspects. . . . The gospel is for all who will truly believe." [16]

Now let us consider the other half of our question. Does the

New Testament sanction the segregation of members of the Christian community along racial or semiracial lines? The answer to this question is clear. Nowhere does the New Testament provide any sanction whatever for the segregation of Christians on a racial—or, for that matter, any other—basis. Christ is the head of a new humanity which gives to believers equal access—without any distinctions of background or advantage—to the divine presence. Though such distinctions may continue to separate believers and unbelievers, they have no place in the Christian fellowship. The barriers that divide men out of Christ disappear once they come together "in Christ," a phrase whose numerous equivalents in Pauline literature include "in the Lord," "into Christ," "in the Spirit," "the fellowship," "the family of God," "the body of Christ," [17] to mention only the most common designations in the apostle's vocabulary for life in the Christian sphere.

Paul's letter to Philemon deserves special attention in this connection; for in this little document—the only extant personal letter from the pen of Paul—the great missionary of the faith comes to grips with this very problem: that of the relationship "in Christ" of men, slave and master, whom the world regards as unequals. To Onesimus and Philemon, the representatives of these respective social classes, Paul bears a common relationship; he has been the instrument of God in their conversion to Christianity—but under quite different circumstances. Philemon became a Christian under the impact of Paul's work in Colossae, and subsequently an influential member of the church in that city (vss. 18-19). After Paul's departure from Colossae, the apostle suffered one of the many hardships he endured for Christ; he became a prisoner for the gospel's sake. Onesimus, the runaway slave of Philemon who had robbed his master before leaving him, visited the incarcerated evangelist, formed a close friendship with him, and subsequently became a convert to Christianity.

Following his conversion, Onesimus, beset with a deep sense of guilt for his treatment of Philemon, seeks Paul's counsel in the matter. Unable to settle this question apart from the consideration of the larger issue of the place of class divisions in the church, Paul weighs the possible solutions to the perplexing problem.[18] At least three such possibilities present themselves for consideration: no fraternity, partial fraternity, and complete fraternity. Which shall it be?

If inclined toward the first alternative, Paul would write: "My dear Philemon, I beg your merciful treatment of Onesimus. Perhaps this is why he was parted from you for a while, that you might have him back as an humble and obedient slave forever." He would urge Onesimus' return to Philemon's service on the same old terms; then, in all probability, he would suggest a period of uncompensated overtime as atonement for his illegal absence. But in actual fact Paul does no such thing. He writes instead: "Perhaps this is why he was parted from you for a while, that you might have him back forever, no longer as a slave but more than a slave, as a beloved brother." (vss. 15-16 R.S.V.) Since Philemon, in at least one sense and in some measure, must henceforth regard Onesimus as a brother, obviously Paul will have none of the "no fraternity" solution.

Now what of the "partial fraternity" solution? If inclined in the direction of this possibility, Paul would sanction a dualistic relationship between Philemon and Onesimus. That is to say, though he might disallow the extension of the unequal status "in Christ," he would still permit it in the everyday affairs of the workaday world. In this event the apostle would write: "My dear Philemon, perhaps this is why he was parted from you a while, that you might have him back forever, both as a slave 'in the flesh' [the Pauline term for the unredeemed life of the everyday world] and a beloved brother 'in the Lord' [a Pauline term for life in the community of believers]." But in actual fact Paul makes no allowance for such dualism. He urges Philemon's acceptance of Onesimus as "a beloved brother, . . . *both in the flesh and in the Lord*"—in other words, both in the community of believers and in the larger community. It's hard to see how Paul could more completely reject the second possible solution.

Indeed, considering the consistency with which he employs the terms "in the flesh" and "in the Lord" in this sense, it's even more difficult to see how Paul could more unequivocally express his suggestion of a relationship between Philemon and Onesimus of unqualified, absolute, and total fraternity. It's not even enough to interpret "both in the flesh and in the Lord" as a demand for the treatment of Onesimus as "a man and Christian," [19] for this implies the separation of the life of the Christian into the compartments of sacred and secular. But in actual fact, Paul does no such thing. Even though Philemon remains in the world, according to Paul, he cannot be of the world. And though he continues to be a participant in the life of the larger community, he must think and feel and act as a member of the household of faith. He will not think and feel and act as a man *and* Christian, he will think and feel and act as a Christian man. He will treat Onesimus as a "beloved brother" both in the household of faith, which embodies believers only, and in the larger community, which embodies believers and unbelievers. "Onesimus will be considered . . . a member of Philemon's family, a full brother. Thus there remains no margin of paternalism, what we have is a total fraternity." [20]

Equally clear, and perhaps even more vivid and explicit, expressions of this same view appear elsewhere in the New Testament. "If ye then be risen with Christ . . . and have put on the new man, . . . there is neither Greek nor Jew, circumcision nor uncircumcision, Barbarian, Scythian, bond nor free." (Col. 3:1-11.) That is to say, the more completely Christ restores us to the fellowship man had with God before the Fall, the more completely distinctions of caste and class will recede into the background.[21]

If one still feels the need of stronger New Testament evidence of Christ's restoration of the redeemed to a relationship of complete fraternity, he does not have to look beyond Eph. 2:11-22. This passage presupposes the segregation of Jews and Gentiles at services of worship in the temple. Loyal Jews erected a wall between the inner court, open only to Jews, and the outer court, open to Gentiles.[22] Thus they tried to prevent contamination of the sanctuary,[23] the boundaries of which did not extend beyond the inner court, by the uncircumcised. According to Josephus' *Wars of the Jews*,[24] the transgression of this taboo carried with it the penalty of death, a fact to which unsuspecting Gentiles were alerted through bilingual inscriptions (Greek and Latin) at regular intervals on this wall. One such inscription, discovered in 1871 on the site of the temple, reads: "No man of another race is to proceed within the partition and enclosing wall about the sanctuary; and anyone arrested there will have himself to blame for the penalty of death which will be imposed as a consequence." [25] We read in Eph. 2:14-19:

But now he . . . [Christ Jesus] hath broken down the middle wall of partition between us . . . that he might reconcile both unto God in one body by the cross. . . . For through him we both [Jews and Gentiles] have access by one Spirit unto the Father. Now therefore

66

ye are no more strangers and foreigners, but fellow-citizens with the saints, and of the household of God.

In other words, the death of Jesus Christ annuls the divisions that heretofore have separated men into superior (fellow citizens) and inferior (strangers and foreigners), privileged and underprivileged members of the community of God's people. If Christian, no matter whether Fiji Island Christians with strange coiffures, black Pygmy Christians, or Indian outcaste Christians, you are brothers in a common family—for we are "all the children of God by faith in Christ Jesus" (Gal. 3:26). And if we are children of a common Father through Christ, then we are brothers to all other Christians, irrespective of race, color, or nationality. And if we are their brothers, dare we offer them anything less than full fraternity in the family of God in Christ? Consider the answer of I John:

We know that we have passed from death unto life, because we love the brethren. . . . Hereby perceive we the love of God, because he laid down his life for us: and we ought to lay down our lives for the brethren. . . . My little children, let us not love in word, neither in tongue; but in deed and in truth. . . . And whatsoever we ask, we receive of him, because we keep his commandments. . . . That we should believe on the name of his Son Jesus Christ, and love one another, as he gave us commandment. (3:14-23.)

In view of the quantity and quality of New Testament passages which voice the plea for full fraternity among Christian brethren, the burden of proof falls on those who question Benjamin E. Mays's declaration: "Even the Christian who excludes non-believers from God's fatherhood cannot logically deny that among believers there should be no barriers based on race, color, or nationality." [26]

67

Summary

The New Testament offers slight comfort to those who approach it in search of a doctrine of brotherhood with which to shore up the cause of segregation.[27] It provides much more comfort for the advocates of the elimination of every sort of invidious discrimination. In fact, it cuts hard against the grain of every single assumption of the argument for the doctrine of a limited or divided brotherhood. It supplies neither argument nor precedent for the restriction of membership on racial grounds, nor for the division of members along racial lines. Quite the contrary, it provides both argument and precedent against the toleration of exclusive practices of this sort—alike at the threshold and in the sanctuary of the household of God. Neither does it prohibit a fraternal relationship between believer and unbeliever. It even sanctions the marital relationship between believer and unbeliever. Nor does it support the proposition that God is Father only of those who so recognize him. But it does support the view that the brotherhood of man presupposes and rests back upon the universal fatherhood of God.[28]

In short, unless distorted to mean what it obviously does not mean, the New Testament view of Christian brotherhood can scarcely be used in defense of the *status quo* in American race relations. And this is true, regardless of where we stand with respect to the church—whether on the inside looking out or on the outside looking in. Since the New Testament view of human brotherhood includes both groups, none of us can deny its relevance to our present situation.

68

CHAPTER V

The Particularism of Jesus

SEVERAL SEGREGATIONISTS HAVE CLAIMED THE GOSPEL EVIDENCES of a separatist attitude by Jesus as a biblical precedent for their position. In view of Jesus' reluctance to associate with certain peoples, they ask, why accuse us of being unchristian for our refusal of fellowship with Negroes? This question raises the whole issue of the legitimacy of their claim to the example of Jesus in support of segregation.

The first three Gospels, it has been noted,[1] contain at least three indications of Jesus' possession of exclusivist tendencies. As soon as Christians base their plea for integration in the demands of the gospel of our Lord, others appeal to one or the other of these passages in support of segregation. This makes it all the more important that we ascertain as nearly as possible the precise attitude of Jesus in this regard. In order to do this we must consider at least three questions. Can we take the separatist texts at face value or, to put it differently, did Jesus really intend this implied limitation of his ministry? If he did intend such a limitation, can it be explained on strategic grounds? Then, to raise the crucial issue, do these passages reveal the typical attitude of Jesus toward non-Jews?

The first of these passages occurs in the Gospel of Mark as the story of the healing of the daughter of the Syrophenician woman (7:24-30), called a "Canaanite" woman in the Matthaean version of the story (15:21-28). The differences in the two accounts[2] do not materially affect its basic significance,

69

for no matter whether a Syrophenician or a Canaanite, the woman is unquestionably a Gentile.[3] And irrespective of the exact words of Jesus' initial rebuke of her for the plea she makes in behalf of her daughter, the text leaves no room for doubt that her Gentile background is the sole cause of his reluctance to grant her request. Indeed, Mark's version very clearly implies what the Matthaean makes explicit in 15:24: "I was sent only to the lost sheep of the house of Israel." (R.S.V.) Rabbinic Judaism frequently referred to ignoramuses and Gentiles as "dogs." [4] Since Jesus takes note of the woman's descent but not of her I.Q., her non-Jewishness must constitute the only ground for his classification of her with the "dogs."

The two replies differ in one fundamental respect. Whereas Matthew's version negates the possibility of a Gentile mission by Jesus, the Gospel of Mark leaves the door open for such activity after the conversion of Israel. But this difference pales into insignificance in face of the sequel in each of the respective versions of this story—in both Gospels Jesus finally grants the woman's request. Neither of the Gospels offers any basis whatever for the denial of the crucially significant fact about the conclusion to this narrative. And that is this: Jesus "did respond to Gentile faith!" [5] In other words, even if we take Jesus' exclusivist statement here at face value, we must still reckon with the fact his inclusivist action canceled its effect.

A second separatist statement by Jesus appears in the Matthaean version of his missionary charge to the twelve. "Go not into the way of the Gentiles," he tells them, "and into any city of the Samaritans enter ye not. But go rather to the lost sheep of the house of Israel." (10:5-6.) Since the parallel accounts of this charge in Mark and Luke contain no hint of any such limitation of apostolic activity,[6] many critics deny that we have

70

the original version of Jesus' remarks in Matthew. However, Walter E. Bundy says, in support of the minority view, that the failure of the church to follow this admonition establishes the case for its utterance by Jesus.[7] Even if we accept Bundy's argument, we still do not have to trace Jesus' advice on this occasion to a separatist attitude. Indeed, two equally plausible explanations lie near at hand. One occurs in the very same chapter of Matthew's Gospel, where the evangelist has Jesus bring his instructions to his disciples to a conclusion with these words: "Ye shall not have gone over the cities of Israel, till the Son of man be come" (v. 23). If these words accurately reflect Jesus' view of the nearness of the end, then his readiness to exclude the Gentiles from the missionary activity of his disciples may be set down to a shortage of time rather than a lack of concern for their spiritual welfare. But even if they do not, it is still possible to offer a perfectly cogent explanation of this delimiting clause in Jesus' charge without recourse to a separatist attitude.

No matter how near or distant the end, argues Philip Mason in defense of the "concentric rings"[8] theory of Jesus' ministry, the spread of the gospel outside Jewish circles would have been greatly retarded if Jesus had not narrowly concentrated his efforts within Jewish circles. In support of this view Mason adds:

Enlightenment must spread outwards from a centre, like ripples on a pond, and that (to change the metaphor to a military one) it is essential to keep one's base secure before venturing on an offensive. It seems clear to me that Jesus did often teach the disciples alone, and that he did regard it as his first task to bring light to the Jews. His time on earth was going to be short; he must make his message clear to those around him and leave it to them to spread the news wider.[9]

71

Oscar Cullmann thinks several of Jesus' disciples may have come from the ranks of the Zealots. This very plausible suggestion raises the possibility that at least these disciples may at one time have been active in insurrections against Rome in quest of an independent Jewish state.[10] Certainly it lends credence to Mason's contention that Jesus' re-education of his disciples took so much time he could not afford the risk of free association with Gentiles. The question is not, Could men of this background win new recruits outside Jewish circles? but, Were the disciples themselves ready for the discharge of any mission to the Gentiles? Considering the probable addiction of at least some of them to the narrow nationalistic ideas of the Zealots, did not their effective prosecution of a Gentile mission presuppose a thoroughgoing transformation of their religious attitudes and outlook? If so, would not Jesus' insistence on an immediate invasion of Gentile territory have succeeded only in alienating his Jewish disciples and antagonizing Gentile candidates for conversion?

The third so-called separatist passage demands only brief consideration. It likewise occurs only in the Gospel of Matthew (the parallel passage in Luke 17:3-4 omits the contemptuous reference). As reported in Matthew, the offensive remark climaxes the discussion of the procedure to be followed in the discipline of disaffected members of the Christian community. If an offended brother remains unreconciled after you have talked with him, first in private and then, in the presence of witnesses, you are to "let him be unto thee as an heathen man [Gentile] and a publican" (18:17). Even if we adopt the unlikely procedure here of denying this utterance to the developing church [11] and treat it as a genuine saying of Jesus, we can scarcely regard it as anything more than an admonition against association with cantankerous Christians. It cannot be taken as proof of Jesus' refusal of fellowship with Gentiles, for Jesus lumps Gentiles and publicans into the same category. Since the same evangelist elsewhere quotes Jesus as saying that publicans will enter the kingdom ahead of the leaders of Judaism (21:31), records his inclusion of a publican in his company of intimate disciples (9:19), and portrays him as the companion of publicans at meal (9:10-13), the interpretation of the disputed portion of this passage (18:17b) as an invitation to follow the example of Jesus would mean just the opposite of what it is taken to mean by the segregationists. That is to say, if the church follows Jesus in its treatment of men, it will make no distinction between Gentiles and publicans. Thus Christians will have to share alike with Gentiles and publicans a common meal, a common task, membership in the same church, and citizenship in the kingdom of God. The very most that can be said for the use of this passage in support of a separatist attitude on the part of our Lord is that Jesus does sanction the excommunication from the Christian community of irreconciliable and obstreperous members. But who would be foolish enough to argue for the immunity of any group, racial, national, cultural, theological, or otherwise, to this spiritual ailment?

We can now answer the first two questions with which the argument for segregation from the teachings of Jesus must come to terms. The first calls for an unequivocal negative: we cannot take the sayings which have been cited in defense of separatism at face value. By the same token, we must answer the second with an unhesitating affirmative: we can readily justify Jesus' concentration of his effort in Jewish circles without recourse to an unyielding prejudice against Gentiles. Indeed, certain considerations seem almost to have demanded a reluctance on

Jesus' part very often to venture outside Jewish circles. His disciples came largely from the ranks of Jews of the exclusivist persuasion. But this fact notwithstanding, their familiarity with the Old Testament and their religious upbringing gave them a decided advantage over the Gentiles in the movement ignited by Jesus of Nazareth. However, even with this advantage, the transformation of zealous Jewish exclusivists into equally enthusiastic inclusivists demanded considerable patience and more than a little time. Considering the fact Jesus had, at most, only three years for this extraordinarily difficult assignment, it is not at all surprising that he delayed his encounter with the problem of what to do with the Gentiles. The amazing thing is that he ever came to terms with it at all—if he did. This takes us directly into our third question, Do the exclusivist sayings in the Gospels betray Jesus' typical attitude toward non-Jews?

Here we do not have to await the examination of the evidence before venturing a negative reply. Simply put, the testimony of the Gospels against Jesus' preferential treatment of men on external grounds is simply devastating. This is true even if we ignore the Gospel of Luke, where Jesus' universalism appears most clearly. Even if we limit our examination to the material peculiar to the First Gospel, the argument for Jesus' regard for each individual man as a person of dignity can hardly be accurately described as less than foolproof. As Mason notes from his study of Matthew, "There is a torrent of evidence, overwhelming, like the rush of water when a dam breaks, all telling against ideas of exclusiveness or superiority, against the world's judgment that those fortunate in wealth or education are entitled to keep aloof from the rest." [12]

The infancy narratives bring Jesus into close touch with non-Jewish people, and apparently to the mutual enrichment

74

of both parties to these scenes. The genealogy of Jesus includes the names of several Gentiles (Matt. 1:1-17), and Babylonian (hence, descendants of Ham, according to the Genesis table of nations; and, needless to add, Gentiles) astrologers join in the celebration of Jesus' birth (2:1-12). Jesus takes refuge (2:13-15) in the land of Egypt (a Hamitic country, according to Genesis, with a Gentile population). The Master grows to maturity in the territory of Galilee, Palestine's melting pot of races, cultures, nations, and languages (2:22-23).

Despite the alleged Jewishness of his Gospel, the First Evangelist records several instances in which Jesus bestows the gifts of his ministry on Gentiles. He heals the servant of a centurion (a Roman, so a Gentile), whose faith he says cannot be rivaled by anything he has seen among the Jews. (8:5-10, 13.) He anticipates the displacement of the children of the kingdom (Jews) by people from the east and the west (Gentiles) in the kingdom of God (8:11). Moreover, even if somewhat reluctantly, Jesus does grant the request of the Canaanite woman (15:22-25).

Despite his Jewish particularism, the Jesus of the First Gospel scarcely ever mentions race or nationality in his list of requirements for appropriation of the life in the kingdom he heralds. He offers it, not to the smug and self-satisfied, but to the poor who mourn, weep, act mercifully, seek peace, and welcome persecution ahead of compromise (5:3-10); not to those who were born aright, but to those who live aright (5:17-20); not to the legalists who never fail to bring their gift to the altar at the appointed time, but to men who put reconciliation with a brother ahead of a date at the altar (5:23-24); not to those who love only their own kind, but to men who love even the people who look on them as enemies (5:43-48). In short, salva-

75

tion in Matthew hinges, not on external gifts open only to the privileged few, but on spiritual gifts equally available to all.

What is more, the people on whom Jesus more frequently and more vigorously pours his wrath than on any others are not, according to Matthew, Gentiles but Jews—a particular group of Jews, the scribes and Pharisees, whom he calls "serpents," "offspring of vipers," and "hypocrites" (23:13-33). Indeed, if we were to single out the people whom Jesus most frequently condemns as a group, it would not be the Gentiles or any segment of the Gentile population, but the scribes and Pharisees of the Jews.

Now, if you will, consider Jesus' parting words to his disciples, as reported in the last chapter of Matthew's Gospel (vss. 18-20). In this final postresurrection incident of which this particular evangelist takes note, Jesus is quoted as saying: "All power is given unto me in heaven and in earth. Go ye therefore, and teach all nations, baptizing them in the name of the Father, and of the Son, and of the Holy Ghost." Even if we follow modern scholars in crediting these words to the early church, they still have tremendous relevance to this whole problem. They clearly indicate the position to which the mind of Christ drove his first disciples. They leave no room for doubt that these disciples very soon came to regard Jesus' warnings against the invasion of Gentile territory as temporary and provisional. In other words, even if Jesus' missionary charge to his disciples before that first Easter did include a directive against activity outside Jewish borders, they felt that the time for the use of this admonition in support of exclusivism belonged to the past. As disciples of the postresurrection era, they felt the time had come to abandon the mandate "Go only to the lost sheep of the house of Israel" for that of "Go ye therefore, and teach *all* nations."

76

CHAPTER VI

The Examples of the Apostles

THE FOLLOWING PARAGRAPHS ARE EXCERPTS FROM A DEFENSE OF segregation in the light of apostolic practice and thought:

We find in the book of Acts three outstanding conversions from the great divisions of the human race. In the eighth chapter we find where the Ethiopian eunuch (a descendant of Ham) was converted. In the ninth chapter we learn of the conversion of Saul of Tarsus who was a Jew (a descendant of Shem). And in the tenth chapter of the same book we learn about the conversion of Cornelius (a Gentile, or descendant of Japheth). So we see that the Gospel of Jesus Christ is universal in its invitation. . . . But the thing that we all need to remember is that we are still the same so far as the physical part is concerned. You never saw a Negro turn white when he was converted. You never saw a Japanese turn into an Indian when he was saved, you never heard of a Jew turning into a Gentile when he accepted Jesus as Saviour. No, indeed, we all still have our same physical characteristics. [All of which would seem only to prove that the Gospel shows no respect whatever for race, despite the rather bizarre conclusion of the author of these words.] And God saw fit to segregate us and all of us need to recognize that fact.[1]

After briefly noting some of the same passages mentioned in the above statement, Gillespie proceeds to lay claim to apostolic support for segregation. He writes:

Since Christ and the Apostles taught the love of God for all mankind, . . . *without demanding revolutionary changes in the . . . social order* [note!], there would appear to be no reason for concluding that segregation is in conflict with the spirit and the teachings of Christ and the Apostles.[2]

So long as we insist on a point-by-point parallel down to the last physical and legal detail, we can find no anticipation in the New Testament of our problem of racial segregation. And for good reason, especially if we follow Culver's definition of segregation as the legal sanction of social distance.[3] Then the failure of the primitive church to declare itself on this issue poses no problem at all. Most of the members of this despised community came from the ranks, not of privileged rulers, but of exploited subjects. Thus the virtual absence of a race problem, as we know it, from the New Testament can be explained quite simply. As Liston Pope notes, "The Hebrews [and the Jews of the first century too] were of the same racial stocks [note his use of the plural!] as the neighbors against whom they drew their lines."[4] The discrimination known to the world of the New Testament was not based primarily on color of skin! [5]

But early Christianity soon ran afoul of the problem of group antagonisms. The effort to determine the distinguishing marks of Christians precipitated intense and bitter rivalries—rivalries every inch as intense and bitter as those kindled in our own time by the controversy over segregation. And this clash did not fail to produce "revolutionary changes in the . . . social order." Indeed, if we follow the precedent of several segregationists in trying to determine the attitude of Jesus and the apostles to the now current practice of Negro-white segregation from their attitude to the then current problem of Gentile-Jew separation, we had better pause for reflection before conceding the validity of Gillespie's argument for the compatibility of segregation and primitive Christianity.

For proof of Christianity's demand for "revolutionary changes in the . . . social order," we do not have to look beyond the answer to this question: Why did the Christian movement, which took its rise within Judaism, so early burst the bonds of its parent faith? Why, indeed, if not because of the rejection by Jesus Christ and the apostles of official Judaism's grounds of admission into the people of the covenant?

These questions carry us into the middle of a problem closely related, alike in basic character and practical consequences, to "the race problem of our day," as one writer so designates it. William D. Schermerhorn so describes the controversy between Jews and Gentiles in his discussion of the "Inward Struggles— Growing Pains" of primitive Christianity.[6] And understandably so, for "the 'race problem' with which the Churches have to deal is not so much a biological as a sociological problem in which theological, cultural and psychological factors all play their part." [7] Despite the unscientific character of this use of the term, it has the advantage of suggesting the similarity "between the problem of race relations and the problems of national, class or other group relations." [8] In this sense, as Schermerhorn has noted, primitive Christianity did have its "race problem." And despite numerous differences between it and our "race problem," called *The American Dilemma* by Gunnar Myrdal,[9] they exhibit numerous similarities. This being so, any examination of the teaching of the New Testament on our "race problem" must begin with a careful look at the solution of the primitive church to the "race problem" among Christians of the first century.

Christianity burst on the scene as a Jewish sect. Its founder was Jewish; its leaders were Jewish; its meeting places were Jewish; its theological and ethical demands were Jewish; in

79

short, the gospel was "born and bred" within the circle and traditions of official Judaism. And official Judaism was a religion for Jews, and only Jews—at least from the viewpoint of the orthodox Pharisees, who defined the standards of the popular Jewish religion throughout the period of Christian beginnings.

When proselytes became members of the Jewish church, they became at the same time members of the Jewish community; more than that, *they became Jews!* As such, they enjoyed "equal rights and duties in all respects with the native born, as is only just, inasmuch as they . . . left country, friends, and kinsfolk for the sake of virtue and holiness.[10] After submission to the threefold initiatory rite by which a proselyte became a Jew, the convert became a member in full standing of the Jewish community, "having all the legal rights and powers *and being subject to all the obligations of the Jew by birth.*" [11] This last phrase means nothing more nor less than assumption of all the requirements of the law; "the authorities say, *if a proselyte takes upon himself to obey all the words of the Law except one simple commandment, he is not to be received.*" [12]

Therefore, despite the unabashed admiration of many Gentiles for Jewish morality, the number of proselytes did not mushroom. Gentiles hesitated to undergo the rite of circumcision, since this would have required them "to obey not only the moral but also the ceremonial Law." [13] Since we have no accurate figures on the number of Gentiles who became converts to Judaism at the invitation of Jewish missionaries, we can only guess at the ratio of proselyte Jews to native-born Jews. But it was, in all probability, somewhat comparable to the ratio of the Negroes who have crossed the color line to the total population of American Negroes. Certainly the number was something less than staggering—for if some Jews looked condescendingly on Gentiles, certain Gentiles repaid the compliment [14] with considerable interest. They resented the high fences with which Jewish leaders had so successfully circumscribed their religious community.[15]

If we want further evidence of Christianity's demand for "revolutionary changes in the . . . social order," we have only to look at official Judaism's calculated efforts to prevent social contact between themselves and their former kinsmen, the Samaritans. Since the law of the Samaritans differed from that of the Jews in several details, Jews, according to strict Pharisaism, could have nothing whatever to do with Samaritans at certain levels and under some circumstances. Especially offensive to them were the discrepancies in the Samaritan regulations governing the ceremonial practice of the Jewish woman during her menstrual period. And they gave vent to their hostility through a pronouncement in which they condemned all Samaritan women as "menstruants from their cradle." [16] And "once the women were presumed to be menstruants, their husbands must be presumed to be defiled by them." [17] If nothing else, this piece of legislation presents us with a rather striking illustration of the limits to which certain Jews went in their attempt to avoid any dealing with the Samaritans.[18]

Official Judaism evolved an "elaborate system of spiritual quarantine regulations" [19] to protect law-observing Jews against association with law-defying Jews. It was a system so elaborate that it offers irrefutable proof of the fact that *the Christianity of the New Testament would have been impossible, indeed utterly inconceivable, apart from a radical break with the social order of the Jewish community.* This latter community, W. D. Davies asserts, felt that "segregation [!] alone could preserve it from extinction; a splendid isolation was the only policy

81

possible!"[20] So its more pious members developed elaborate rules for the avoidance of social contact with the ritually impure. They banded together in small groups, not wholly unlike early Methodism's class meetings, for mutual encouragement and cultivation. Two of their membership requirements vividly illustrate their rigidly exclusivist policy. One calls for the refusal of entrance as a guest into the house of a lax Jew; another for the denial to such a person of admission into one's own house.[21]

The prevailing Jewish view of the law of Moses in the first century allowed ample room for the development within Judaism of a new sect. But only if its members limited their social contacts to people who observed the regulations of the moral and ceremonial law. One can only guess as to what would have happened if Judaism had permitted intimate social relations with people who ignored the regulations of the law. But we can be virtually certain it would have introduced a veritable wave of volcanic changes in the social order of the Jewish community. Therefore, we ask the simple question, What was the attitude of Jesus and the apostles to the lax Jews (frequently called "sinners"[22] in the New Testament, especially in the Gospels), the Samaritans, and the Gentiles? Did they seek them, or did they spurn them? Did they welcome them, or did they eschew them?

It made little practical difference to the orthodox Jew of that day as to which one of the three categories the excluded individual belonged. The ground of his exclusion was the same in any case. However, since the probability of firsthand contact decreased in accordance with the order in which they are last mentioned in the preceding paragraph, we shall examine their treatment at the hands of Jesus Christ and the apostles in this sequence.

All the Gospels record Jesus' disregard of the taboo, especially at meal, against contact with Jews who did not observe the law—people such as the publicans and sinners. He praises the "woman of the city, who was a sinner," for her anointment of him in the home of a Pharisee—and this was done despite the Pharisaic prohibition against the toleration of such intimate contact with a person of this sort (Luke 7:36-50 R.S.V.). On another occasion, when his critics upbraid him for "eating and drinking with publicans and sinners," he identifies his ministry to just such people as his major responsibility in life (Luke 5:32). Then, as if to heap ridicule on insult, he joins a party of such persons at table (Luke 15:2) and, on one occasion, even invites himself to become a guest in one of their homes (Luke 19:2-10). And these incidents are probably only isolated illustrations of the general pattern of Jesus' entire public ministry. At least, the frequency with which his enemies assail him for his friendship with such people would seem to suggest as much. He must have spent a great part of his ministry in the company of people who, by the standards of strict orthodoxy, stood outside the pale of official Judaism. As a consequence, since "Pharisaism . . . acted on the principle of avoiding contact with the wicked, . . . Jesus as the friend of publicans and sinners became notorious." [23] By the same token, some of the apostles also achieved notoriety. Or to put it more accurately, the apostles fell heir to the same notoriety; they—or, at any rate, a few of them—were born into it.[24] They were born into the homes of Jews who did not observe all the regulations of the law.

If anything, the Samaritans fared even better at the hands of Jesus and the apostles. And this, even though the relation—or the lack of it!—between Jews and Samaritans in the first century

83

approximated, at least in attitude and intensity of feeling, contemporary expressions of racial pride. Despite a common ancestry, they avoided each other (John 4:9). Yet Jesus transgresses this custom time after time. When Samaritan hostility forces his abandonment of the plan to spend the night in one of their villages, he refuses the frantic plea of two of his disciples for the exaction of vengeance; quietly and without fanfare, he takes another route (Luke 9:51-56). Another time, on receiving a very different sort of welcome, he turns the hospitality of the Samaritans into a two-day visit in one of their cities (John 4:40-42). Again, in a startling revelation, Jesus divulges to a Samaritan woman his anticipation of a religion that will render obsolete the long standing debate over the relative positions of the chief shrines, respectively, of the Jews and Samaritans (John 4:20-24). Then, in what must be viewed as the most striking evidence of Jesus' disapproval of the anti-Samaritan attitude of contemporary Jews, note his readiness to make a Samaritan the object of special praise. As in the case, for example, of his praise for the gratitude of the Samaritan, the only leper of the ten, who bothered to thank him for his restoration to health (Luke 17:12-19)—but even more in his use of a Samaritan as *the exemplar of a greater love than that of the priest or Levite* (Luke 10:30-37). And here, at least by implication, Jesus raises a question that must have shaken the Jew, proud of his contempt for Samaritans, to his bootstraps: If a Samaritan can mirror the love and concern of the holy God, how can you justify your demand for the separation of your people from his people?

The primitive church wasted little time in the formulation of its answer to this question. And that answer was no less clear and unequivocal than prompt. Repudiating the anti-Samaritan attitude of their fathers, the members of that church turned to

Samaria in search of new recruits for the gospel. Unable any longer to justify separation from those who had sought and found union with God in Christ, they sent Peter and John into Samaria "to complete the work" so ably begun by Philip. With this, in what we can scarcely regard as the introduction of anything less than a "revolutionary change in the . . . social order," *they launched a movement for the integration of people from whom, for the better part of five centuries, they had remained segregated!*

This brings us to the issue that split Judaism down the middle, the question of the admission of Gentiles. Even before the appearance of Jesus of Nazareth on the scene, Jewish missionaries raised questions of earth-shaking proportions concerning the admission of Gentiles.[25] But this debate never altered the official policy of Judaism one iota; as erstwhile, Gentiles could win recognition as practitioners of Judaism only if they became Jews. However, as one might well expect, considering Jesus' disregard of the Jewish proscription of association with publicans, sinners, and Samaritans, his followers were destined to evolve a new and "revolutionary" Gentile policy. Two issues claimed the lion's share of attention in this development: (1) the grounds of admission into the Christian community, and (2) the subordination of Gentiles (and, for that matter, others) in the life of the Christian fellowship.

Jesus' teaching and ministry reveal numerous instances of his anticipation of Gentiles among his followers (Matt. 8:10; 28:19; Mark 3:8; 7:24; Acts 1:8), but debate of the grounds of their admission into the ranks of Jesus' disciples does not become heated until after the Resurrection. The first clear hint of the controversy appears in the Acts account of Stephen's speech before the council. The text of this speech leaves no room for question as to the ground of the arresting party's accusation. He spoke "blasphemous words against this holy place [the temple], and the law" (6:13). But of what did his blasphemy consist? Did he, as Caird [26] contends, credit Jesus with putting "an end to both Torah and temple"? Or did he, as G. H. C. Macgregor[27] suggests, plead the case of "a more liberal type of Judaism, which emphasized the moral rather than the ceremonial side of the law"? It makes little difference, at least for our purpose. For even on Macgregor's argument, he defended a position incapable of incorporation into the official Judaism of the first century. In any event, by the canons of the religious authorities of his day, he committed blasphemy in defending the right to membership in the holy community of those who had not submitted to the rite of circumcision, symbolic of their acceptance of "the yoke of the kingdom." Stephen, regardless of whether we identify his audience as Greek-speaking Jews or Gentiles,[28] did anticipate "Paul's assertion of a distinctively free, Gentile Christianity." [29] Moreover, he inaugurated a "revolutionary change in the . . . social order"; unless, of course, we can accept a lynching as a part of the established order.

This change, due in great measure to Paul's refusal to settle for any sort of compromise, becomes standard Christian policy within a single generation after Jesus' death. The climax comes in the solution to the controversy over the joint participation of circumcised (Jewish) and uncircumcised (Gentile) Christians in the fellowship meal which included the Lord's Supper. No matter what the solution, the Christian movement can scarcely fail to lose favor in the eyes of one of the two parties. If it goes on record for the permission of this meal, many Jews will think twice before risking participation in another such gathering. And for good reason, since by this action they would both excommunicate themselves from the Jewish community and, in large measure, close the door on their opportunity for the evangelization of fellow Jews. On the other hand, if the apostles require submission to the initiatory rite of Judaism, Gentiles will resist with as much force the overtures of the Christian evangelists as they do those of the Jewish evangelists. Which shall it be?

The New Testament contains two versions of the solution to this problem. The first reports a compromise. The authorities make certain concessions to the strict party, but stop short of the indispensable prerequisite of the conservative party (Acts 15:24-29). Apparently this solution had the effect—if it was ever really adopted!—of pleasing exactly nobody. Indeed, from the viewpoint of official Jewry, this solution was no compromise at all; it was outright surrender! At any rate, even if put into effect for a time, it was a very short time. Paul tells us in Galatians of the willingness of James, Cephas, and John, pillars of the Christian community in Jerusalem, to recognize him and and Barnabas as ministers of "the gospel of uncircumcision." He also relates that Peter, who had been appointed to "the apostleship of the circumcision," ate with the Gentiles of Antioch before the appearance in that city of the members of the strict party from Jerusalem. (2:1-12.) The Acts account of the conversion of Cornelius offers additional evidence for the victory of the liberal party in this struggle. Indeed, as Dibelius points out,[30] Luke relates this story for the express purpose of demonstrating the notion that the idea of receiving Gentiles into the church without requiring their submission to the law originated, not with Peter, nor yet with Paul, but with God.

Though James did his best to avoid giving offense to the conservatives, it proved to be a fatal mistake. No matter if he himself did continue to observe the regulations of strict Judaism, *the Jewish Christians of Jerusalem simply could not tolerate his tolerance.*[31] It was not enough for them that he should set a good example[32] in this matter. He had to punish all who did not follow that example. So long as he did not, he was still "open to serious criticism from the Jewish side. He acknowledged the legitimacy of a Gentile Christianity which did not keep the Law." [33] Therefore, despite James's own strict observance of the Jewish law, the high priest Ananus took decisive action against James and his party of Jewish Christians. Apparently it resulted in James's death by stoning. Following this brief episode of violence, the Christians of Jerusalem abandoned that city and took refuge in Pella across the Jordan,[34] where Jewish Christianity "dwindled into a small sect as unimportant in the life of the Church as it was insignificant in the life of the Jews." [35]

The futility of the compromise of the party of James demonstrated the impossibility of invigorating a world movement within the framework of a nationalistic faith. So the demise of James brought the church face to face with as clear-cut an either/or as any with which it has ever been confronted in all its history. Would it cling to the law and remain a Jewish sect? Or would it surmount the law and become a world faith? Unable to do both, it did the latter. It spurned the segregation of Gentiles in favor of separation from the Jews. In so doing it introduced some quite "revolutionary changes in the . . . social order." We have already seen how it compelled the Christians of Jerusalem to seek refuge across the Jordan. But even more significant than this, it drove such a wedge between the two religious systems, Jewish and Christian, that the followers of both had to choose "the Law or the Gospel, Sinai or Calvary, Moses or Christ." [36] They could no longer have both. *Thus ended the change where-*

by the social order, Jewish only, became two social orders, Jewish and Christian. (The reader may decide for himself as to whether this change was revolutionary!)

The primitive church answered the question of the subordination of Gentiles in the Christian fellowship in an equally clear and unmistakable way—so clearly, in fact, there is no need here for a detailed examination of this aspect of the problem. Two illustrations will suffice. The first finds the widows of the Hellenists complaining of the practice of invidious discrimination against them in the distribution of alms. The leaders of the Jerusalem church, after considering the matter, appoint seven deacons to attend to such details, lest such discrimination be perpetuated. The prominence of the men whose names appear on the list of appointees indicates the church's determination to see to it that the widows of Hellenists got their fair share. Several of these men appear elsewhere in the New Testament as missionaries to non-Jews. Thus we have one instance of how the church's leaders dealt with a case of flagrant discrimination. They betrayed no disposition either to ignore it or to leave its resolution until some more convenient season.

The second passage relates the solution of one New Testament writer, the author of James, to the budding problem of segregation along economic lines in the Christian fellowship. He castigates kowtowing to the wealthy. He calls "church ushers" to account for their practice of reserving the choicest seats for the economically privileged, while providing only footstools or standing room for the less fortunate.

If ye fulfil the royal law according to the scripture, Thou shalt love thy neighbor as thyself, ye do well: but if ye have respect to

89

persons [which means, to show partiality in judgment, by having regard for the outward circumstances of men], ye commit sin, and are convinced of the law as transgressors. For whosoever shall keep the whole law, and yet offend in one point, he is guilty of all. (2:8-10.)

This leaves only one question still to be answered on this point. Did the church condemn the manifestation of "respect to persons" on racial grounds? Since the Jew-Gentile question represents the New Testament's nearest approximation to a race problem, we have only to ask, Did the church of the New Testament period discriminate between Jew and Gentile? It did not, according to the testimony of Acts. Acts mentions several Jewish synagogues in which Jews and Gentiles worship together on a nonsegregated basis (at Thessalonica, 17:4; at Berea, 17:12; at Corinth, 18:4 ff.; at Ephesus, 19:9-10), and portrays the worship of Jewish and Gentile Christians in several local churches (see 11:20; 13:1; 13:43-48) on an integrated basis, without any hint whatever of any sort of discrimination. Along with the suggestion of a similar practice among the Christians in the chief city of the Roman Empire (Rom. 2:17; 11:13), Paul adds his personal testimony on this whole question. And while it may be going too far to wring from the following statements of that testimony his support of "a nonsegregated church in a nonsegregated society" (the goal of many American denominations), surely they can scarcely be interpreted as less than a plea for "a nonsegregated church":

For as many of you as have been baptized into Christ have put on Christ. There is neither Jew nor Greek, there is neither bond nor free, there is neither male nor female: for ye are all one in Christ. (Gal. 3:27-28.)

Wherefore remember, . . . ye . . . who are called Uncircumcision [Gentiles] by that which is called Circumcision [Jews] in the flesh made by hands: that . . . Christ Jesus . . . hath made both one, hath broken down the middle wall of partition between us. (Eph. 2:11-14.)

Lie not to one another, seeing that ye . . . have put on the new man, . . . : where there is neither Greek nor Jew, circumcision nor uncircumcision, Barbarian, Scythian, bond nor free: but Christ is all, and in all. (Col. 3:9-11.)

Summary

In teaching "the love of God for all mankind," Jesus Christ and the apostles wrought numerous revolutionary changes in the social order. And where did they meet the stiffest resistance to their cry for a change? Precisely at the point of encounter between Jews and Gentiles. But they defied all tradition in their solution to this problem. They said, in effect, "It's time for a change!" They wrought a change too—or, to put it more accurately, a revolution! They said that segregation had to go, even though the end of segregation within the Christian community would surely mark the growth of the clamor for the separation of the disciples of Jesus from the children of the law. And segregation went.

PART III

What Are the Implications of Biblical Faith
for the Christian Approach to Segregation?

Introduction

THE VALUE OF THE BIBLE AS A GUIDE IN THE STUDY OF THE
problem of race hinges in great measure on the expectation with
which we approach it. As indicated in the preceding pages, it
provides little comfort for those who come to it in the expectation of finding props with which to shore up the cause of segregation. It offers just as little comfort to the people who approach
it in quest of a set of guiding principles for the implementation
of integration. The Bible cannot properly be described as Christianity's substitute for Dean and Rosen's *A Manual of Inter-
group Relations*.[1] Though the Bible suggests the possibility of
the relative approximation of the reign of God in history, it
does not provide us with a set of blueprints for its actualization,
approximate or otherwise.[2]

However, if we come to it in search of ethical and theological
considerations of relevance for our approach to the race problem,
we shall be rewarded beyond our highest expectation. For the
Bible yields, to all who come to it in this spirit, something more
and superlatively better than a particular solution to a particular
problem. It reveals to us an understanding of the origin, nature,
and destiny of man from which we can derive relevant considerations for the resolution of this—and, indeed, every other—problem in human relations.

But this understanding cannot be narrowly explicated in terms
of the biblical doctrine of man, and apart from all other considerations. If this comes as a shock to modern man, may he
stand reminded of the fact that the writers of the Bible were not

modern men. They would have scoffed at his humanistic scorn of the supernatural; they could not conceive of man apart from God. Except as they began with God, they despaired of the possibility of either rightly knowing or wisely guiding man. And they would have been equally at a loss to understand the dogma of rugged individualism; that is to say, neither could they conceive of the individual apart from the community to which he belonged.[3] Except as they viewed man in terms of his membership in and responsibility to the people of God, they could not begin to understand either his predicament or his mission. In short, to derive biblical concepts of special relevance to problems in human relations calls for a close look at the biblical view, not only of the dignity and responsibility of man, but also of the character and purpose of God and the identity and mission of the people of God.

Perhaps we should pause here to note the impossibility of deriving "the biblical view" from a numerical tabulation of "proof texts culled indiscriminately from its pages."[4] At least we Christians, without denying the faith from which we derive our name, could never attribute equal authority to all portions of the Bible. Inasmuch as the biblical record contains numerous instances in which poets, prophets, and apostles of limited moral and spiritual maturity and sensitivity obscure both the character of God and the nature of his requirements, we must correct their words in the light of the Incarnation.[5] That is to say, as Christians, we must correct the words of Holy Writ, as everything else, by the *Word Made Flesh*, and not vice versa. Therefore, with Christ as "the touchstone" for the elucidation of the permanently valid concepts of the biblical revelation,[6] let us now examine the theological and ethical teachings of the Bible which are most relevant to the question of race.

CHAPTER VII

The Character and Purpose of God

THE BIBLICAL WRITERS NEVER RAISE THE QUESTION OF GOD'S existence. Not once do they stoop to the demonstration of the logic of belief in God as the surest clue to discovery of the whence, why, and wherefore of finite existence[1]—but they have their theological problems as surely as if they had been sophisticated agnostics. As a matter of fact, their basic problem on this score, just as ours, concerns the discovery of the relevance of belief in God to the control and conduct of human life.[2] We might explicate their solution to this problem in a variety of ways. Perhaps we can best do it by means of a brief summary of the chief roles in which the authors of the Scriptures cast God in the drama of biblical religion.[3]

The Creator of All

The authors of Holy Writ everywhere assume the creation of the world by God. Yet they betray only passing interest in this phase of divine activity for its own sake. Not because of any doubt of the need for God as the answer to the question of the whence of the cosmical order. But for precisely the opposite reason: they saw no room for such doubt; they could as little doubt the necessity of God as creator as they could doubt the reality of creation. In other words, creation became a problem for them at precisely the point where it ceases to be a problem for the modern scientist (that is, not as a human being, but as a scientist!). The concern of the scientist as scientist ends with consideration of the work of God as creator as the answer to the ultimate theoretical question. But they launched their inquiry in search of the answer to the ultimate practical question. They were little exercised by the question, How can we most adequately account for the world and its inhabitants? Almost as little, in fact, as they were much exercised by this question: If God really be the creator of us and our world, what difference does this belief make in the way we should think and feel about ourselves? Needless to add, the answer to this question calls for an examination of the religious situation of the people who elicit the biblical reminders of the work of God as creator.

The first biblical writer to draw all the key implications of monotheistic religion, the author of Isa. 40–55, makes more of the doctrine of creation than any other biblical writer. But not because he has a highly speculative mind. Rather, as Reinhold Niebuhr notes, he introduces the idea of the majesty of God as creator of the world "to reinforce the concept of the divine sovereignty over historical destiny." [4]

And how the faith of the people of Israel stands in need of such reinforcement! Their ancestors came into the land of Palestine with a sense of God-given destiny. They looked forward to the establishment of a mighty empire, and the development within its borders of a holy people. Though this hope eluded them, they transmitted it to their children. So it passed from generation to generation to generation, century after century, until the fall of Jerusalem, the destruction of the temple, and the deportation of the Judahites. The Jews in exile find themselves dumbfounded by the gaping chasm between their lofty hope and sorry fate. They awaken momentarily from their spiritual blackout, but only to fall again into the throes of morbid despair. And there they remain, too proud to cry and too skeptical to

hope. They glimpse a faint ray of hope in Persia's sweeping vic-
tories—but they dare not pin their hopes too securely to the
coattails of ascending Cyrus. After all, how can they be sure that
he will not turn out like other emperors?

To be sure, the author of Isa. 40–55 does not seem to anticipate such an eventuality. But neither does he ground his message
of comfort in his high confidence in Cyrus. Nor does he base it
in his lofty estimate of the character of the Israelite people,
though he acknowledges their suffering to be greater than their
sin (40:2). He turns instead to the work of God in creation.
Though the exiles can trust neither themselves nor the nations,
they can trust their God, for he is the Lord of creation. He has
sustained them in the past, and he will restore them in the future.
Here the prophet's own words are too matchless to risk a mere
summary of his ideas:

Why sayest thou, O Jacob, and speakest, O Israel, My way is
hid from the Lord, and my judgment is passed over from my God?
. . . Hast thou not heard, that the everlasting God, the Lord, the
Creator of the ends of the earth, fainteth not, neither is weary?
there is no searching of his understanding. He giveth power to the
faint; and to them that have no might he increaseth strength. (40:27-
29.)

And who are they who are "faint" and "have no might"? They
are the children of Israel in a strange land: a people with no
political power and very little freedom; a people with very little
economic stability and slight hope of increasing it; a people with
only fragments of an ecclesiastical order and small hope of
cementing them. But Israel has every reason in the world to
anticipate a great and glorious future, for despite all her woeful
ineptitude—politically and economically and ecclesiastically—

she boasts an indestructible dignity. At long last Israel comes to a full awareness of the futility of unconditional trust in anything and everything earthly and temporal. Israel finds herself, her true self, in a tremendous act of self-abandonment. And this act has two stages. It begins with the bold proclamation of the Creator's absolute independence alike of his creation and creatures (48: 12 ff.), and it ends with the humble acknowledgment by the people of Israel of their complete dependence on God for everything they are and have and hope (51:8-13).

As in the case of Gen. 1:1–2:4a, the prophet's doctrine of creation must be interpreted as "a theological commentary on the meaning of existence." [5] And that meaning can be stated quite simply. The dignity and the hope of the human creature are as strong—or as weak!—as the ties that bind him to his heavenly creator. Or to put it differently, man has no earthly reason to anticipate a coming good time in history except as he rests his confidence in that Goodness which lies outside earth and time and history.[6] However, once he abandons himself wholly into the care of his Creator, he comes by a power that dwarfs into pitiful insignificance the pomp and splendor of even mighty Babylon. The grateful acknowledgment of man's dependence on his creator furnishes him with an antidote for the temptation to despair: a faith that time cannot destroy, nor tragedy dull.

Israel's God has the power to "form the light and create darkness" (45:7). Indeed, he is the Lord of creation. This being so, so long as she remains humble and obedient, Israel has no excuse for falling victim either to bleak pessimism or morbid despair.

But what if men approach God with the opposite attitude? What if, instead of viewing their dignity as something wholly conferred, they treat it as something partially deserved? What if, instead of coming to God with a confession of weakness and a plea for mercy, they come to him proudly to exhibit their great achievements and make their bold demands? How do the biblical writers interpret the significance of the belief in God as creator for people of this sort?

Simply put, they view such people as pretentious and self-deluded frauds. They see no hope for man unless he empties himself of all pride in everything made. Only thus can man have a proper, or indeed, any sort of meaningful, relationship with his Maker.[7] No matter what the man-made anchor of his devotion, be it economic privilege (Amos 6:4 ff.), national glory (Amos 1:1-3:14), ecclesiastical splendor (Jer. 26; 27), worldly wisdom (I Cor. 3:19), or, for that matter, moral uprightness (Mark 10: 17-18), it will fail him in the moment of encounter with his Creator.

If now you or I should ask, What shall I say to such a man? the Old Testament's greatest prophet furnishes us with this ironic suggestion: "All flesh is grass. . . . The grass withereth, the flower fadeth: . . . surely the people is grass. The grass withereth, the flower fadeth: but the word of our God shall stand for ever" (Isa. 40:6-8).

Man cannot properly acknowledge God as creator except as he renounces his concern for the approval of anything and everything that is not God.[8] Although the Creator is quick to impart significance to those who do not claim it for themselves, he is just as quick to deny the significance of those who do claim it for themselves.

Now to sum up the matter. The biblical writers remind two kinds of people of the role of God as creator: self-renouncing individuals[9] standing on the threshold of despair, and self-centered individuals reminding the world and the Lord of their magnificent gifts and glorious achievements. In effect, to the former they say: "Now that you have discovered the futility of the search for security in the life and world of the creature, turn to your Creator in repentance and faith, and find true security, a security the world can neither give nor take away." For the latter, however, they have no such comforting assurance, but only this solemn suggestion: "Lift up your eyes on high, and behold who hath created these things. . . . Even the youths shall faint and be weary, and the young men shall utterly fall: But they that wait upon the Lord shall renew their strength" (Isa. 40:26-31). In short, to us all they say: "If you seek security in the humble acknowledgment of God as creator, nothing will be able to take it from you. By the same token, if you seek it in the proud elevation of anything else, not even your creator will be able to give it to you."

The biblical interpretation of the significance of faith in God as creator raises questions of vital importance for people on both sides of the current crisis in race relations. Here are some of the questions it raises for the advocates of segregation as the Christian solution to this problem: How can you possibly justify the attachment of so much importance to differences in the color of human skin? Do you not thereby deny the notion, stemming from the biblical view of God as creator, that the only difference of really decisive religious significance is that which separates, not one group of men from another, but every man from his creator? Since you are as dependent on your Maker for all you are and have and hope as the man who *inherited* parents of another race, what right have you to treat the color of your skin as a ground for favored (or, if you insist, *separate*) treatment at the hands of men?

102

By the same token, lest they confuse a limited good with the ultimate good, the advocates of integration do well to ask themselves these questions: Do you ground your plea for integration in the equality of men among men or in the equal dependence of all creatures on their Creator? Do you remind the members of all races that only in the humble acknowledgment of their dependence on God can they achieve and preserve a secure freedom for the members of any race? Do you look on the Creator as a useful ally in the struggle for integration? Or do you think of your support of integration as one aspect of your creaturely obligation to your creator?

How you answer the above questions makes a difference. No matter what side you take in the controversy over segregation, you can hardly claim biblical support for your stand unless you are willing and happy to let the Creator be God.

The Redeemer of All

The notion "that God should create man and then be careless of his welfare," E. L. Allen writes, "why, that would make Him not God at all, but a devil!" [10] With this statement, I think it safe to say, practically all the writers of the Bible agree. From Genesis through Revelation, with three or four possible exceptions, they identify the will of God as creator with the will of God as redeemer.[11] But not all of them provide us with equally significant clues to the redemptive concern at the heart of creation.

Indeed, from the very beginning, the Christian gospel has subordinated all other clues to the one revealed in the life, ministry, crucifixion, and resurrection of our Lord, called by one writer "the Christ Event." [12] Then, to narrow the field still further, it has found the center and focus of this event in the

103

Crucifixion.[13] "The Cross is," as Allen notes, "the starting-point of Christian thinking about Christ" [14]—and, by the same token, of our search for a clue to the nature and work of God as redeemer.

If troubled by the question, What kind of God? we have only to go to Calvary to find the biblical answer on which the church laid her foundations. The Cross represents our guarantee that God carries human sin with a heavy heart; that the petty pride of man does not leave him untouched and unmoved; that our rebellion costs him greater pain than anger.[15]

Calvary marks the Bible's most vivid and eloquent clue, we have said, to the meaning of Christian faith. But not because it claimed the life of the best man who ever walked this earth. If this exhausted the meaning of the Cross, we might dismiss it—to be sure, with a frown—as a sad commentary on human nature. But, alas, there is more to it than that. For "God was in Christ" [16]—even on the cross—yea, especially on the cross; and there he suffered, not only with man and as man, but also because of and for man. And this, not merely to reveal the high cost of sin, but also to recall man to the fellowship for which the Creator made him.

"Primitive Christianity took sin seriously, but that was not the last word. God took it seriously, and was doing something about it." [17] And how good for us he did! For if he had not, we—all of us, including those of us who have no doubt as to our moral fitness, yea, most especially us!—would be doomed, hopelessly and irrevocably doomed. As Paul saw so clearly and stated so neatly, this is why the Cross becomes to some men a "stumblingblock" and to others "foolishness" (I Cor. 1:23). There is no redemption for those who will have none of any governor's charity, not even if that governor happens to be the chief executive of the universe. If not saved by the sheer grace of their Redeemer, they simply will not, because they cannot, be saved otherwise. Either they become reconciled to God through his seeking and forgiving love, or they remain in a state of sinful separation. "For by grace are ye saved . . . and that not of yourselves: it is the gift of God: not of works, lest any man should boast." (Eph. 2:8-9.)

Certainly this biblical doctrine raises serious questions for those Christians among us with a desire for the preservation of segregation. God receives us into fellowship with himself on the sole condition of our grateful acceptance of his prodigal generosity.[18] This being so, how dare we insist on additional prerequisites for the joint participation of other men with us in a branch of this fellowship? If God ignores such qualifying factors as sex, race, and nationality in his gracious offer of forgiveness, can we make a legitimate claim to membership in the fellowship of the forgiven if we respect such factors? If we insist on the right—which the only person (God) who stands in no need of forgiveness chooses not to exercise—to play favorites among the candidates for forgiveness, must we not plead guilty to the charge of ingratitude? Do we not thereby lay ourselves open to the charge which a certain man brought against his proud and self-righteous neighbor, when, on catching sight of him walking down the street, he exclaimed: "But for the grace of God, there goes God"?

And it raises questions of no less significance for those Christians among us in favor of integration. For if we look on our emancipation from race prejudice as proof of superior virtue, do we not thereby deny the doctrine of salvation by grace? And if God's forgiveness knows no limit, can we lightly and indiscriminately dismiss all segregationists as expendables in the holy war for first-class citizenship for all our people? At this point it might be well for us to pause for a little spiritual stock-taking. Do we ever trace our own thoughtless words or inconsiderate deeds to an unhappy childhood, the influence of domineering parents, a severe headache, or upset nerves? If so, is it not possible that some of our bigoted neighbors might be able to do the same, and with no less justification, for their prejudice against members of another race?

Integrationists must guard against premature elation over the discovery of no basis in the biblical view of salvation for either the theory or practice of segregation. They do well to remind themselves of at least one additional fact about the biblical view of salvation. It does not entitle them either to the rejection of the persons or the refusal of fellowship with segregationists. Though the support of segregation may constitute proof of the inability either to understand or appropriate salvation in the biblical sense, the support of integration cannot be accepted as proof either of its acceptance or appropriation. While the Bible provides considerable support for both the theory and the practice of integration—at least of the members of the people of God—this fact must not be viewed as a ground for boasting. God is our redeemer, and not we ourselves.

The Judge of All

The key writers of the Bible do not hesitate to cast the God whom they know as creator and redeemer in the role of judge. Indeed they devote so much space to the treatment of God's performance in this role [19] that we must sharply limit our discussion of this phase of divine activity. We can only take a very brief look at three elements in the biblical view of the judgment of God which have the most serious implications for the question of segregation. Note how all three call attention to what most men would regard as the *surprising* character of divine judgment.

The biblical writers surprise us, first of all, by anticipating the judgment of God at an unexpected time. The great prophets of Israel, men like Amos and Isaiah, exercise the least restraint in their proclamation of doom during the periods of the nation's greatest prosperity.[20] While the activity of both these prophets fell within a half century of Samaria's capitulation to Assyria, that catastrophe seemed utterly remote at the time of their inaugural visions. It had been a long time since the political and economic health of the nation had been half so good. The king's economic and political experts greeted the masses with glowing promises. They assured them of even greater political power and an ever-expanding economy. They could interpret their good times as the sign of nothing, if not, still better times.

But not so in the case of Amos and Isaiah. They brought to their task peculiar skill in the rare art of reading the signs of the time from the viewpoint of the divine will. And because they did, they found in their analysis of Israelite life no basis at all for the current wave of optimism. Amos could see nothing promising in a prosperity which, instead of leveling, heightened the barriers between class and class. Isaiah found it equally hard to see any hope for a national policy that flitted back and forth, like a silly dove, from one lover to another.

Neither man hesitated to express his opinion for all to hear. When men use their blessings to magnify rather than mitigate the problem of need, according to Amos, they had better watch out. For their peace and calm may well be the harbingers of calamities alike in nature and among the nations. When nations put their trust in horses and chariots, according to Isaiah, trouble

107

is just around the corner. The Lord is a jealous God, and he will not tolerate any rival, no matter whether this rival bases his claim on political influence or economic affluence.

Why did these prophets afflict prosperous Samaria and comfortable Judah? Was it merely because they were comfortable and prosperous? No. It was because their comfort and prosperity had betrayed them into a false estimate of life. They had allowed their concern for an abundance of the good things of life to blind them to the fact that the good life does not consist in an abundance of things. So Amos and Isaiah proclaimed bad news in good times.

Who can make sense of such action? Anybody who reads human history or, for that matter, human nature through the eyes of biblical faith. For men of this faith, from Amos in the Israel of Jeroboam II to Reinhold Niebuhr [21] of our America, have never been willing to accept material prosperity at face value. They have never lost sight of its ability to awaken in men the sinful pride with which they have the broad and easy way to the destruction of respect for God as judge.

Do not we citizens of prosperous America, whether for segregation or integration, stand in need of this prophetic warning? If we attempt the defense of segregation on the ground that American Negroes enjoy a higher standard of living than any other members of their race anywhere else in the world, do we not thereby repudiate the prophetic denial of prosperity as proof of God's favor? Have we not turned what to Jesus and the prophets was a sign of approaching danger into a proof of divine blessing? On the other hand, if we seek integration from no higher desire than to see all men enjoy an equal chance on Commerce Street, have we not come within a hair's breadth of crowning mammon the god of our cause, if not of our lives?

And is the same not true of the comfortable people who, though they believe in integration, leave its implementation to their great-grandchildren?

Regardless of our position with respect to the Mason-Dixon line, we do well to recall the reluctance of the biblical writers to equate prosperity and piety. Despite the display by certain modern judges of a lenient attitude toward men of position, the Judge of the Bible betrays no such bias. He judges the prosperous as well as the poor; yea, if anything, he judges the prosperous even more severely than the poor.

The biblical writers surprise us, in the second place, by the audience to which they most frequently address their reminders of God's action as judge. It does not consist of mockers and unbelievers, but it consists of the people who are most conscious of the need for God's exercise of judgment. In fact, they are so conscious of man's need of God as judge that they do not hesitate to hand down God's verdicts for him.

Our Lord's parables of the tares (Matt. 13:24-30) and of the dragnet (Matt. 13:47-52) illustrate the scorn with which Jesus and the prophets greeted such presumption. Each of these parables capsules this idea: Of all the judges in the universe, none can be trusted to separate the wicked from the righteous, the goats from the sheep; for this we need—indeed we must have—the Judge of the universe. God alone can be trusted justly to decide this issue.

Like the church of today, that of apostolic times attracted a motley crowd. People joined it from different motives, with different attitudes, and in the strength or weakness of a wide variety of moral attainments. "Why," many asked, "if the kingdom of God came to earth in Jesus Christ, are we still plagued with half-converted churchmen?" Some of their neighbors, not content just to debate the issue, took action. They took the matter, or rather the offending members, in hand and threw them out of the church.

Some of the saner members of the church proposed a less drastic solution to this very touchy problem. These sought and found their solution in the above parables. The parable of the tares postpones the separation of the wheat to the harvest, a symbol here, as in Jewish literature, of the final judgment. Jesus' parable of the dragnet illustrates the same point, for the dragnet gathers fish of every kind, size, and condition. Those who spread the net of the kingdom must "not draw too many distinctions. . . . God, in his good time, will judge; it is the prerogative of Jesus and his followers to offer salvation and forgiveness." [22]

Hand in hand with this deferment of judgment goes the recognition of the inadequacy of all merely human judges. Where the cases call for verdicts of such ultimate significance, mere men have no real competence. Here Jesus implies a stern rebuke of those of us who, in our haste to usher in the kingdom of God, insist on a "pure church" [23] composed only of the perfect. The point is that there's really no live option to a church of the imperfect. Either we concede the validity of an imperfect church, or we deny the validity of any church. And for a quite simple reason—one so simple, in fact, we are likely to ignore it. At the same time, however, it's so serious we cannot afford to ignore it. That reason is:

We are tares: only by a self-righteous pride could we claim to be a weedless field. . . We should be ruthless with the evil in ourselves, but cautious in our dealings with evil in others—since our eyes and understanding are both short; and we should be grateful to God's patience that he does not "liquidate" us. [24]

110

So long as God does not purge us, how happy we should be to leave the purge of our neighbors to God!

If only we could find a proper respect for God as judge, how it would alter both the form and the tone of the questions with which we approach the problem of racial tension! No longer could we vote the liberal line with one eye on the political power of Harlem and the other on the reaction of the ADA and NAACP. And we would not ask, "What would the abolitionists of the nineteenth century say about our fence-straddling approach to desegregation?" Neither could we any longer vote the conservative line with one eye on the political power of Dixie and the other on reactionary newspapers. Nor would we ask, "What on earth would our slave-holding ancestors have to say about our toleration of integrated schools?" As with one voice, we all should ask instead, "Lord, what wilt thou have me to do?" (Acts 9:6). Then, as a consequence, both segregation and integration would cease to be such powerful and prevalent forms of idolatry in American life.

Now for an illustration of what it means to face this problem in humble acknowledgment of God as judge. After a long chat, two Christian friends, one a Negro, and the other a white man, went their separate ways along the street. A friend of the white man, aware of his father's strong belief in white supremacy, asked him, "What on earth would your father think if he had seen you chatting with a Negro?" "To tell you the truth," he answered, "I haven't given it the slightest thought. I was too busy wondering what my Father in heaven would think if I had refused."

This brings us to consideration of the third surprising feature in the biblical portrait of God as judge. Jesus provides us with the classical illustration of this point in his parable of the last

111

judgment (Matt. 25:31-46). Note the surprise with which both groups receive the verdict. The righteous are as amazed by their acceptance as are the wicked by their rejection. Just as the former did not care that it was the Son of Man to whom they ministered, so the latter did not know that it was the Son of Man to whom they refused to minister. If they had only known, they would have been glad to feed him when he was hungry, give him to drink when he was thirsty, and visit him when he was sick or in prison. But then they would have ministered to him from ulterior motives, and not just because he was a human being in need of their help. They would have come to his aid because, as a divine being, he could do far more for them than they for him.

By the same token, the Judge identifies the righteous by their indifference to the identity of the people to whom they give succor. They see them only as human beings in need of help. They ask no questions about their color, creed, caste, or character. Nor does Jesus leave much room for doubt as to the inference we are to draw from this parable. The conclusion is clear. If we would win the verdict of the righteous, we must be equally indifferent to questions about the color, creed, caste, and character of the hungry, thirsty, sick, and imprisoned people who come to us in need.

But the wicked did not know! And neither do we. We do not know, indeed we cannot know, just what would happen to us or to them if we should become ministers to the underprivileged people who are hungry for justice, thirsty for opportunity, sick at the thought of having to raise their children in slum-blighted ghettos, and in prison to constant reminders of inferiority. Neither do we know, nor can we know, just what would happen to us or to them if we should become ministers to the more privileged people who, sick with pride and in prison to ancient prejudices, are hungry for greater privilege and thirst after more power, not for their neighbors, but for themselves. But our inability to ascertain the outcome will not keep us from ministering to either group. Certainly it will not deter those of us for whom the Judge of the biblical writers reserves a favorable verdict. For he does not reserve this verdict for the people who persist in doing good for the sake of the outcome. He reserves it for the people who persist in doing good regardless of the outcome.

The Lord of History

How can you know what God did in the beginning? Or how can you be so sure of what God will do at the end? Such questions may stump us, but they would not have disturbed the authors of biblical faith. They were sure of how God had acted in the past and of how God would act in the future because they were sure of how he was acting in the present. They did not come to their faith in God through the study of "the beauty of the earth." Nor after a futile search elsewhere for the clue to the whence of history. They began, instead, with a view in which God marches "onto the stage of history as the Chief Actor." [25] And they ended there too. Whatever else they had to say on any subject can justly be regarded as commentary on their faith in God as the Lord of history.[26] And history as seen through the eyes of the people who made it!

The biblical writers, even when they are looking backward to the ancient past or forward to the distant future, always have their eyes firmly fixed on the present. When they go back to the Exodus for a reminder of Israel's dependence on God, they do so in the hope of eliciting Israel's acknowledgment of her

113

present responsibility before God. A similar motive underlies their predictions of forthcoming doom at the hands of a holy God. They predict the overthrow of a wicked Israel in the hope of effecting Israel's transformation into a righteous people. Then there will be no occasion for Israel's overthrow.

They do not view men as the helpless pawns of either an inexorable past or of an inevitable future. Their reminders of God's previous actions in behalf of his people are always prompted by a concern for the grateful acknowledgment of this indebtedness to God in the daily life of the here and now. God's "claim to ownership . . . of land, life and substance is never an old claim, but a claim incessantly renewed in historical and timely event." [27] Biblical anticipations of the future are always tentative for precisely this reason. The aim of such predictions is "not to unveil an inevitable future, but to alter the variable element in the present situation, the action of men, in relation to the constant element, the will of God, and so to alter the resultant situation." [28]

It is highly important to recall that the biblical writers treat the moral character of God as the one constant among the variables of human history. It is even more important to observe that they see this as the only constant in human history. All else in human history can and does vary. This marks the one and the only invariable factor with which men must come to terms in the ebb and flow of human existence. And they must come to terms with it constantly. They will experience renewal as a result of a closer approximation of the divine character. Or else they will suffer judgment as the penalty for departure from it.

Practically all the biblical writers believe it possible to predict the future of men and nations on the basis of their present character. Their maxim is this: As a people's relationship is with God, so will their fortune be. If they be related to God as an obedient servant to a sovereign Lord, they have every reason to expect the best; in due season, if they faint not, they will be rewarded. By the same token, if their relationship to God be that of a proud rebel, they will be judged accordingly. In short, those who have a proper relationship with God shall be given even greater security, and those who do not shall have taken from them what little security they now seem to have. To be sure, in the last stages of the development of biblical faith, it is clearly recognized that history gives to some people less and to others more than their due. But even these writers do not abandon the belief that the Judge of all the earth both can and shall do right by the children of men. They simply defer the realization of perfect justice to another world and another life.

The biblical writers interpret God's dynamic control over history in terms consistent with the divine character. Consequently, they lend no support whatever to the notion that geographical, national, ecclesiastical, or, for that matter, any other kind of boundaries can or should be fixed. No generation is bound by the deeds, or misdeeds, of a previous generation. The lordship of God and the operation of justice appear in the Bible as two sides of the same shield.[29] "Biblical ethics . . . appears within a framework of concrete, personal decisions."[30] And these decisions have "far-reaching consequences."[31]

Every generation in every nation has to decide for or against righteousness, for or against him who is the God of righteousness. And in every nation [or, we could add, individual], . . . the selection against righteousness means self-destruction.[32]

Now for a look at the bearing of this faith in God as the Lord of history on the race problem. Here there's neither much room for question nor much reason for pause. Since justice and righteousness underlie God's control over history, we have only one question to ask ourselves. What would constitute a just and right relationship among the races of mankind? Or rather, since justice and righteousness in biblical faith are what they are because God is what he is, What is God's will in the current racial crisis? This is the crucial, indeed the only important, question. While it is important to recognize the operation of divine judgment in history, it is even more important that we recognize the divine character as the standard of judgment. The important thing is that we come to see that "it is with him alone, and with him as he really is," [33] and not with northern liberals or southern reactionaries, that we must come to terms. And this, not merely at the end of history, but in the flow of history. For just as the Bible sees God as one anxious to pour blessings upon an obedient people, so it presents him as one ready to punish the disobedient with inevitable destruction.[34]

The biblical writers accentuate the danger of settling for anything less than God's will in any crisis, great or small. When men do it, they insist, they put themselves as well as their cause in jeopardy. Indeed, since a holy God cannot accept an unrighteous people without denying himself, they invite rejection at the hands of the sovereign lord of history.

Summary

The biblical view of God offers little encouragement to those who treat their concern for public worship as an excuse for their failure to work for the betterment of the human situation—certainly not as much as it offers those who insist that the worship of God and love of neighbor go hand in hand. If the Bible's stress on God's work as creator, redeemer, and judge reminds us of the severe limits of human action, the biblical emphasis on God's role as the Lord of history just as clearly accentuates the crucial significance of human action. If the biblical doctrine of creation highlights the folly of human arrogance, the biblical view of God's control over history spotlights the danger of human irresponsibility. And if the former warns us against the presumption of thinking we can do everything, the latter precludes the possibility of thinking we can do nothing. The works of the God of the Bible permit "no description apart from a clarion call to repentance and conversion, even on the part of the one who is dissecting them." [35]

The biblical writers, because they worship a dynamic God, confront us with a dynamic view of history.[36] They do not interpret history as a theatrical performance to which we can contribute only as an audience. They see it rather as the arena of the action of the sovereign Lord of "life, death and destiny." [37] They see it as the sphere in which God accepts and rejects men and nations on the basis of their response to his gracious offer of faith and freedom in fellowship. Not that human action in any way conditions the fact of God's reign. God reigns unconditionally. Regardless of human action, God reigns. But human action can and does alter the manner of God's reign. How he shall reign, whether in grace or judgment, hinges on our response to his call. But regardless of our response, God reigns forever and ever.

117

CHAPTER VIII

The Dignity and Responsibility of Man

BECAUSE SOME ELEMENTS OF THE BIBLICAL VIEW OF MAN HAVE only a remote and indirect bearing on the question of race, we shall consider here only those aspects of the biblical view of man which have the most immediate and direct relevance for our approach to this problem.

A Creature of God

Our generation has produced a whole galaxy of experts in the analysis of racial attitudes. If we favor segregation, we experience little difficulty in tracing the history of our prejudice on American soil. The same goes for those of us who prefer integration. We can trace our spiritual ancestry to Lincoln and back again. Nevertheless, our study of the problems of race does not suffer from too much analysis. Quite the contrary, we fail to carry our analysis back far enough. If occasionally we get as far back as Lincoln or Lee, we usually remain content to stop there. Much too often we allow our analysis to come to an end before it takes us back to the beginning. Only rarely does it take us back to the time when God created, not the "American" man, not the "white" man, not the "privileged" man, but simply man.

The biblical treatment of the subject of man makes no such mistake. It takes us all the way back. It begins at the beginning. It takes us back to the point when, prior to the origin of race or nation, creation awaited a call to order from the Creator. Perhaps this fact accounts for the strong insistence by practically all the really outstanding students of the Bible on the principle of human equality. Maybe it also helps to account for the repudiation of the principle of human equality by some of the people who disregard the Bible. At any rate, unless we ground our plea for human equality in the recognition of man as the creature of God, we shall be hard put to it to justify it.

Apparently the framers of the Declaration of Independence recognized this fact. They did not contend for the proposition "all men are equal" as "a self-evident truth." They sharply qualified their assertion of human equality. The "self-evident truth," as they saw it, is not that "all men are equal" but that "all men are *created* equal." If they had wanted to be even more accurate and at the same time more biblical, they would have said instead that "all men are equally created." But be this as it may, the defense of the doctrine of human equality apart from the biblical faith in God as the creator of all men presents us with a formidable task.

If inclined to doubt this statement, we have only to examine the almost universal assumption in the workaday world of human inequality. Everywhere men assume, not the equality, but the inequality of men to be self-evident. Boxing promoters assume the physical inequality of men; they would not think of matching a flyweight against a heavyweight. Educators assume the mental inequality of men; they even use intelligence tests for measuring the variation in native capacity. Social workers assume the economic, cultural, and social inequality of men; they have even devised criteria for spotting delinquency areas on the basis of such inequality.

In the face of such numerous and indisputable facts to the contrary, how can we possibly contend for the principle of human equality? As a matter of fact, we cannot. The plain facts

119

of the human situation demonstrate exactly the opposite. Men differ markedly, are indeed grossly unequal, in physical endowment, intellectual capacity, social advantages, cultural achievements, and in many others ways. These are the bare and cruel facts. Obviously, therefore, we must look beyond, or rather behind, the facts if we would make a case for human equality. Since we cannot defend this plea as a matter of fact, we must contend for it, if at all, as a matter of faith. And this faith must be grounded in a religion which "contends for equality in being, . . . not in performance; equality in essence, . . . not in capacity. . . . The necessary insistence . . . on the equality of all men finds its grounding ultimately in religious faith." [1]

It's really quite difficult to take seriously the argument for human equality apart from the faith which sees man's relation to God as that of creature to creator. Almost as difficult, in fact, as it is to take seriously the argument for human inequality on the basis of this faith. For no matter how great their achievements, men of this faith know that they can never exceed the potentiality of their God-given capacities. Though they may erect an ever so beautiful human edifice, they never cease to see themselves as unqualified, utter and hopeless debtors to God for the foundation on which they raise it. Consequently, they cannot take themselves seriously enough to encourage the belief that they have the right to lord it over other men. Nor can they take seriously a like claim by any other man—regardless of the weapon with which he seeks to implement the assertion of his right to special privilege or immunity. They know that the person who lays heavy stress on the social, national, racial, physical, political, intellectual, moral, or religious differences among men has overlooked the one difference that dwarfs all others into comparative insignificance. They have learned that there's really only one crucial difference in life. And this is not the difference which separates the Assyrian from the Jew, nor that which separates the suave cosmopolitan from the swarthy farmer, nor even that which separates the saint from the sinner. The only really crucial difference is that which separates the Creator and creature. This is the only difference which brings us face to face with different levels of existence—the one wholly independent and unconditioned, and the other wholly conditioned and dependent.

The Bible indicates this difference through its refusal to speak of the "holiness" of any person save God. Too often we treat this word as mere shorthand for the moral purity of deity. We can avoid this error by recalling that the Bible does not apply this term in its original sense, which means "to be separate," to man. Man could not be holy in this sense and remain man. Indeed, belief in God's holiness is only the other side of the denial of man's holiness. The biblical assertion of God's holiness, therefore, implies the recognition and worship of God as wholly independent of and completely different from anything and everything created. Sometimes the Bible makes this distinction through the use of the words "spirit" and "flesh" as semitechnical terms. "Spirit" stands for power, independence, stability, and immorality; and "flesh" for weakness, dependence, frailty, and mortality. "God is a spirit." (John 4:24.) "All flesh is grass and . . . the grass withereth." (Isa. 40:6-7.)

The importance of this aspect of the biblical doctrine of man can scarcely be exaggerated. So long as the ordinary, run-of-the-mill man of a different race remains the standard of comparison, many men can boast of their inequality. Yea, they can boast even of their superiority and their right to boast or rule. But how different when they begin to measure themselves against

121

their Creator. Then they have little difficulty in seeing their dependence on him for all they are and have, be it ever so little or ever so much. Once men grasp the true significance of the worship of God as creator, they have little trouble in grasping the significance of the principle of human equality, an underlying presupposition of every democracy. Indeed, once men come to this view of the relation between God and man, they can readily see why democracy is not only possible but necessary. Democracy is possible because God created man in his own image. (Gen. 1:27.) By the same taken, democracy is also necessary. It is necessary because man, even though God's creature, never completely escapes the temptation to usurp the place of God.[2]

The Bible sees men as equals, not in native capacity, not in physical development, not in cultural progress, not in social poise, not in political know-how, not in spiritual maturity, but in more fundamental and ultimate respects. Men are equal in their dependence on God for their place in creation; they are totally dependent on God for their place in creation. Men are equal in their dependence on God for their membership in the covenant; they are totally dependent on God for their membership in the covenant. Men are equal in their dependence on God for their anticipation of a glorious future; they are totally dependent on God for their anticipation of a glorious future. Therefore, cries the prophet Jeremiah:

Thus saith the Lord, let not the wise man glory in his wisdom, neither let the mighty man glory in his might, let not the rich man glory in his riches [nor, might we add, "neither the colored man in his color nor the white man in his whiteness"?]: but let him that glorieth glory in this, that he understandeth and knoweth me, that I am the Lord which exercise lovingkindness, judgment, and right-

122

eousness in the earth: for in these things I delight, saith the Lord. (9:23-24.)

A Free Person

Assuming the constancy of the divine character and God's unbroken lordship over the sphere of human existence, history would be a perfectly straight line, devoid alike of ups and downs. But history, we all know, cannot be so neatly graphed. The line of history exhibits sudden, sharp, and, occasionally, strange curves.

Why so much variation in the course of human events if a God of reliable character be both the author of life and the Lord of history? Since God, the Lord of history, has allowed the rise and growth of segregation, why should we feel obligated to view it as a problem for us to solve? Why not leave it to God?

This question raises no serious difficulty for the majority of the authors of biblical religion. As if guided by a single prompter, they lay the lion's share of the blame or credit, as the case may warrant, at the door of men. They trace a rather precise, sometimes a little too precise, moral connection between the character of men and the course of history.[3] Almost all of them interpret both natural and national calamities as expressions of divine judgment on sin. Similarly, they interpret natural and national benefits as so many instances of God's reward of faithfulness. Therefore, despite their unshakeable faith in God's sovereign control over history, they do not cast history into a severely deterministic mold. Rather, they see it as a drama in which the Divine Director finds himself, because he chooses to be, sharply limited by the abilities and attitudes of the members of his troupe. Not that they would go so far as to say that men write the script of the drama God directs. But neither would

123

they be content merely to say that men act the parts of the script God writes. In a deep and vital sense, to a degree unthinkable in many contemporary secular philosophies of history, they cast men in the dual role of author and actor in this spatiotemporal drama—but never so as to rob God of his solitary grandeur as the alpha and omega of the entire performance. In other words, they take human freedom seriously without in any way impugning or impairing the divine sovereignty.

Here we are concerned with the doctrine of human freedom only in a very limited dimension. In fact, only insofar as it confronts each new generation with a demand for life-shaking and life-shaping decisions. The members of every generation can make such decisions; they must make such decisions; they cannot escape the consequences of such decisions. This threefold assumption provides the clue to delineation of the relevance of the biblical view of human freedom to problems in social ethics.

The Bible betrays more than a passing awareness of the stifling influence of immoral society on moral men.[4] Yet almost all the authors of biblical faith find in each generation more room for the exercise of freedom than it uses. They offer little encouragement to the people in quest of a hiding place from God. Indeed, they appear almost cruel in the manner in which they pull the rug from under such people. Once men begin to treat their heritage as a hopeless moral and spiritual deficit, the biblical writers take them to task without hesitation or reservation. Unable to contain their disdain for this freedom-denying, responsibility-begging perversion of faith, they pull no punches in their attack on its disciples. Neither do they sanction the cry of those who plead the inheritance of an out-of-joint time as an excuse for inertia. Never again shall any Israelite, Ezekiel declares, have occasion to use this proverb:

124

"The fathers have eaten sour grapes, and the children's teeth are set on edge" (18:2-3). No matter how bad the situation, we can act. Circumstances never become so bad that we, by proper faith and action, cannot work an improvement, if not in the circumstances, at least in ourselves.

If possible, the Bible betrays an even harsher attitude toward the people who treat their heritage as an inexhaustible treasury of moral and spiritual capital against which they can draw at will without any obligation. It flays the people who imagine themselves to be inevitably implicated in the benefits incurred by previous generations. The authors of biblical faith denounce them in terms of unqualified rebuke. They castigate them as the victims of a wicked and dangerous delusion—and without respect to persons. They make no exceptions; they make no concessions even to the people who employ a high doctrine of the Christ as an excuse for low living or a static faith.

The author of Hebrews reflects some awareness of the danger inherent in the removal of Christ from the human sphere. He qualifies his elevation of Jesus to divine status with a vivid description of the humanity of Jesus. His moral and spiritual victory did not come about, we are reminded, through any special privilege or immunity. Men cannot trace it to his failure to participate in our uncertain life and inescapable death. They must ascribe it, instead, to the fact that he met the imponderables of our precarious existence without falling victim to sin or despair.

Then, lest we overlook the danger of assuming that we can appropriate his supremely expensive victory at no cost or risk to ourselves, the writer calls Jesus "the pioneer of . . . salvation" (2:10 R.S.V.) . Thus he suggests the impossibility of preserving the faith without at the same time renewing it. Pioneers do not

125

eliminate the need for hard-working settlers; they merely clear the wilderness for the prosecution of fruitful labor. Especially is this true if the end in view be the household of faith. Unlike property, faith cannot be passed from one generation to another in fixed quantities. We cannot build on the faith of the saints unless we build with the faith of the saints. And to all the people who think otherwise, and live accordingly, the Bible addresses them, through John the Baptist, in this call to repentance: "Bring forth therefore fruits worthy of repentance, and begin not to say within yourselves, We have Abraham to our Father" (Luke 3:8).

No matter how rich our heritage, we must act. Circumstances never become so good that we, by complacency and inertia, cannot work the ruin, if not of our situation, at least of ourselves.

Men can act. Man must act. And they must act now. What is more, they must be prepared to accept the consequences of their actions, both now and later. Paul emphasizes this notion through his recurring stress on "the wrath of God." This term in Pauline thought does not support, as sometimes is assumed, the tendency to look on God as a vengeful despot. Paul employs it, rather, as a figure of speech for the rejection men bring on themselves through the constant disregard of God's gracious offer of salvation. Indeed, seldom does Paul mean any more by it than this: God's mercy in no way cancels out the freedom and responsibility of man.[5] That is to say, despite God's great mercy and forgiveness, he does not drag men, against their will, kicking and screaming into his kingdom. If they choose, they can reject God and his kingly rule. But if and when they do, they must also accept the consequences of such choices, for here choices and consequences come wrapped in the same package.

On this aspect of the judgment of men the biblical writers

speak as with a single voice. This marks a rather surprising fact, considering their differences in interpretation of other aspects of the judgment. For they cannot agree as to the time or place of the judgment; indeed, they even differ in their identity of the judge. But on this single item they present a unanimous front: regardless of when and where the judgment falls, men will fare well or ill according to the merit or demerit of their choices.

God confronts each generation of men with a demand for decision and, from it, there is neither escape nor reprieve. If men decide against God *now*, they cannot know the joys of heaven *later*—any more than they can recall the decisions of those who went *before*. *Before* is irrevocable time; we cannot recall it, no matter what we do or how hard we try. *Later* is irrelevant time; we can neither advance it nor postpone it, try as we may to usurp God's prerogatives. *Now* is inescapable time; here we change both the *before* and the *later* and, depending on the direction in which we do it, find or lose life for ourselves and our society.

God's time for us is *now*. With the God of all creation and the Lord of history calling us to judgment, the alarm for decision has sounded. And we must answer this alarm, *now*. Today we have the freedom and the responsibility to choose the divine purpose for ourselves and our society. We are not only experiencing history; we are making history.

This facet of biblical thought, if it has any validity at all, undercuts our readiness to shift the burden of our problem to the shoulders of some other generation. If segregation is wrong, we alone must bear the responsibility for the perpetuation of a segregated society. While we may trace its existence to the sinful choice of a previous generation, we cannot justify its perpetuation on this ground. If perpetuated beyond this generation, it will be due chiefly to the sinful choice of this generation. If we would, we could reduce the evils of segregation.

Neither can we excuse our inaction in anticipation of the reforming zeal of the coming generation. For while they must bear the full weight of responsibility for what they choose to do with segregation if they inherit it, we must bear the full weight of responsibility for whether or not they inherit it. God holds us responsible for the society we hand down to the next generation—for if we would, we could change it.

A Social Being

The biblical view of man precludes even the serious consideration of the philosophy of the society-scorning individualist. Men of the self-made and self-sufficient variety fare no better in the Bible than in real life. The authors of biblical religion take them seriously only long enough to rebuke them for the assumption of an independence no man can rightfully claim or possibly exercise. They know man as a member of a community of equals. Let us see how they develop this idea.

The Old Testament most clearly implies this idea in the writings from which we derive our material for what one writer calls "the prophetic criticism of life." [6] Even though Israel's great prophets only rarely delineate their expectations of men in positive terms, we have little trouble in defining their concept of a healthy society. They imply this quite clearly, even if after a negative fashion, in what they identify as the marks of a diseased society. Let us take Amos as our example.

Amos flatly contradicts the popular view of "the day of the Lord." Whereas the great masses of Israelites look forward to it as an occasion for joy, Amos anticipates it as an occasion for weeping. He sees no possibility for the deliverance of Israel

128

from utter doom. This in itself poses a real problem for the secular readers of Amos. They have a hard time seeing how Amos could possibly anticipate early disaster for Israel at the zenith of her political and economic power. Then, as if to doubly complicate the problem of such interpreters, Amos does not arrive at his dire prediction as the result of his study of the military and political power of Israel's international enemies. He bases it rather on his analysis of Israel's domestic life.

Amos does not fear Israel's external foes half so much as the glaring evidences of internal weakness and decay. This becomes clear from his roll call, one by one, of the offenses for which they must soon experience retribution: the treatment of human beings as the mere tools of economic ambition, the idolization of the plutocrat, the cultivation of an insatiable taste for ornate and expensive furniture, the use of unbalanced scales, the practice of deceit in the return of measures, the criticism of sabbath observance because of its interference with trade, the trimming of the professional services of religion to the size of the worshiper's purse (see Amos 2:6 ff.; 3:9 ff.; 5:24; 6:4-6; and 8:5 ff. for the basis of this summary of his criticism of life). For these reasons, Amos declares, "the day of the Lord" will bring judgment rather than joy, adversity rather than prosperity.

The New Testament offers us the positive side of this picture in its delineation of the life of him who is the revelation, yea, the Incarnation, of life—the life that is life indeed. According to the author of Luke, Jesus interpreted his public ministry as a sort of running commentary on the text:

The Spirit of the Lord is upon me, because he hath anointed me to preach the gospel to the poor; he hath sent me to heal the brokenhearted, to preach deliverance to the captives, and recovering of sight to the blind, to set at liberty them that are bruised, to preach the acceptable year of the Lord. (4:18-19.)

These verses clearly imply that true religion, though it is rooted in the vertical relationship that exists between man and God, will stamp a redemptive imprint on the horizontal relationship that obtains between man and man. Certainly Jesus' public ministry provides us with ample material for the complete documentation of this position.

Does our worship of God carry with it an unrelenting demand for the alleviation of poverty, the emancipation of the enslaved conscience, the restoration of sight to men who have been blinded by prejudice, hate, and strife, or the deliverance of men from conditions that stifle their search for moral and spiritual meaning in life? If not, we can scarcely defend it on biblical grounds. Both testaments deny the possibility of rightly worshiping God as Father so long as we ignore or hate our fellow men, brethren with us in his family, whom he wills that we should love and help. "Not every one that saith unto me, Lord, Lord, shall enter into the kingdom of heaven; but he that doeth the will of my Father which is in heaven." (Matt. 7:21.)

The Bible sees man, not as an individual among other individuals, but as "an individual-in-community." [7] Accordingly, it treats the inequalities of man, not as a sanction for invidious discrimination, but as evidence of the necessity for viewing life as "a mutual relationship deriving from inequality." [8] Such inequalities should work a healing, not a divisive, influence within the human family. When viewed rightly and used properly, the superior gifts of privileged men, be they mental or physical, economic or political, will not become an excuse for widening the gap between the haves and the have-nots Instead, they will so use them as to make the abundant life equally available to all. In keeping with its strong emphasis on the inescapably social character of human existence, the Bible confronts us with a somewhat atypical version of the ideal man. Unlike Mr. America, he is not "a man among men"; like the Good Samaritan, he is "a man for mankind."

Numerous people have been impressed by some of the "proofs" of the unreadiness of many Negroes for integration. Here are a few of the most frequently mentioned examples: they have more illegitimate children and are guilty of more sexual irregularities; they produce more than their share of criminals and juvenile delinquents; they live in rundown houses; they live on fats and starches.

We shall not question the truth of such charges. Considering the extent of their separation from decent schools, a fair wage, good housing, and a host of other privileges, it would be surprising, indeed incredible, if the Negroes of America, all of a sudden, could match us whites, privilege for privilege, and appliance for appliance. Few of us whites are so dull that, if given a generation's jump on Negroes, we cannot break the tape ahead of them in the race for commercial and cultural advantage. The Negroes cannot afford to give us so great a handicap. Neither can any other people.

But dare we demand it? If equal privileges would enable them ultimately to rival us in achievements, dare we plead their inferior achievements as an excuse for the denial to them of equal privileges? Quite obviously, it all depends on whose scriptures serve as the basis of our view of man. If we adopt Machiavelli's *The Prince* as our Bible, we can go one up on the exponents of the "separate but equal" doctrine. We can insist on inequality as well as separation. But what if we derive it from the Bible of the Christian Church? Well, that's a different story, one with a *just* as well as a happy ending.

A Responsible Person

In view of what we have just said about the social dimension of human existence, we cannot discuss man's responsibility apart from consideration of his duty to his neighbor. By the same token, since both he and his neighbor owe their origin and destiny to God, we must likewise take account of God's will in our attempt to clarify man's duty to men. This calls for the addition of a qualifier to our description of the biblical version of the ideal man. No longer can we describe him simply as "a man for mankind." We must henceforth speak of him as "a God-directed man for mankind." This means we must look at two questions in our effort to define man's duty to men. What constitutes the norm of ethical conduct? How does it help us, if at all, in deciding how we should think about and act toward our neighbors?

G. F. Moore answered this first question when, in his description of Jewish ethics, he wrote that "the supreme principle and motive of moral conduct in Judaism" [9] is the santification of God. Why should the Israelite be good and do good? In order that, so the Old Testament would answer, he might thereby praise and glorify the God of Israel. For long centuries, under all sorts of conditions, the prophets ignited the faith of Israel with their demand for the imitation of God. Where they left off, ethically speaking, Jesus began and ended. As surely as any of Israel's great prophets, Jesus grounds his moral demands in the plea for the imitation of God. The conclusion to the opening chapter of the Sermon on the Mount (Matt. 5:48) presents us with an interesting illustration of this point. Readers of the

132

King James Version of the Bible have sometimes been perplexed by the demand in this verse that we be "perfect." But textual critics have rescued them with the assurance "upright" would probably better translate the Aramaic word that was probably used by Jesus. But does this rob the demand of its sting? Is the impossible and unattainable thereby brought within our grasp? Well, let's see what happens if we omit the terrifying word. "Be ye therefore . . . ," we would then read, "as your Father . . . in heaven. . . ." No matter how we translate the adjective in this verse, we are still confronted by the demand for the imitation of God. *The goal of human striving must still be determined, as elsewhere throughout the Bible, on the basis of the divine character.*[10]

In the light of the foregoing answer to our first question, we have simplified the problem raised by our second question. If we would find how we should feel and act toward men, we have only to ask how God feels and acts toward men. Indeed, we can further reduce the scope of our search. Since we read the Bible from a Christian standpoint, we have only to ask, What does the New Testament, and especially the Gospels, understand God's attitude toward men to be—especially if those men are oppressed or underprivileged?

The Gospels portray God as a Father who loves the unrighteous as well as the righteous, who bestows his gifts on the good as well as the evil, who suffers for the disobedient as well as the obedient, who deals with his children on the basis of need rather than merit, and who, with unquenchable concern and indestructible love, seeks the salvation of all. Now, if we should undertake the revision of our attitude toward others in conformity with that of such a God, just what would this mean in practical terms? It would mean that our righteousness would not entitle us to a hostile, much less hateful, regard for the wicked. Since the God of Christ hates no one, neither can the imitator of this God. By portraying God as one who loves all, irrespective of moral and spiritual achievement, Jesus' demand for the imitation of God enlarges the boundaries of moral obligation to universal proportions. In short, as the imitators of the God of Christ, we shall both covet and seek the abundant life for all God's children—especially for those who do not deserve it (see Luke 15).

This brings us to consideration of one of the most vexing questions of the entire New Testament. What prompted Jesus to say that harlots and publicans would enter the kingdom of heaven ahead of the people who obeyed the law of Moses to the last detail? Could it have been the feeling that the people who keep God's commandments but ignore his children are farther from the imitation of God than the people who love his children but transgress his commandments? Jesus' association with the outcasts of society offers strong evidence in favor of some such assumption. Indeed, if we derive the demands on us of the imitation of God from the example of Jesus, we can hardly stop short of a radical revision of the whole basis of our association with men. No longer can we justify the choice of friends or companions solely on the basis of similar backgrounds and common interests. We shall henceforth be more concerned about *their* needs than our interests. We shall also harbor a greater concern for the realization of their potentialities than proof of the compatibility of our backgrounds.

The Gospels call us to the worship of a God who puts great emphasis on the need for and value of vicarious faith. The Matthaean version of Jesus' cure of the one sick of the palsy pre-

134

sents us with an interesting illustration of this point. "And Jesus seeing *their* [the men carrying the sick man's bed] faith said unto the sick of the palsy; Son, be of good cheer; thy sins be forgiven thee." (9:2.) These words leave the clear impression that the faith of men can affect the health of their neighbors.

This suggestion of the power of vicarious faith should pose no stumbling block for us moderns. After all, from men in every field of social service, we are constantly being bombarded with reminders of the necessity for its demonstration. Authorities in crime and juvenile delinquency never weary of telling us that we cannot greatly reduce antisocial behavior until we have liquidated the environments which breed antisocial attitudes. Psychiatrists frequently send patients home to recuperate from minor mental disturbances on the assumption that friends who love them will do more to expedite their recovery than experts who do not. Ministers everywhere recognize the importance of a strong supporting group as a key factor in the achievement and maintenance of social health. Educators have long attached great importance to the presence on campus of a "cultural atmosphere" or "academic climate." Experts in almost every field of social endeavor now follow Jesus in the ascription of healing power to vicarious faith or prevenient love. They insist that the best way to bridge the gap between the cultured and the uncultured, the privileged and the underprivileged, the fortunate and the unfortunate, the saint and the sinner, is for the cultured, the privileged, the fortunate, and the saintly to love their opposites over to their side of the street. Of course, Christians would have to add to this a somewhat rhetorical plea. Since God spared not even the Cross in his quest of us sinners, how can we possibly imitate this God if we shut off, not only our schools and our restaurants, our hotels and our churches, but also ourselves from other sinners for whom he died?

The biblical view of man's responsibility may not enable us to sustain the charge of falsehood against the people who say of the few Negroes whom they have known: "They are dirty, . . . unmethodical, . . . unpunctual, and irresponsible; give them a cowhouse to build and the wall will not be straight; give them a start in business and they will waste their capital, and so on." [11] Factually speaking, these people may be quite right. Biblically speaking, however, their observation, even if factually correct, would still be morally irrelevant. The God of the Bible does not trim his love to fit the facts of an unpleasant situation. He broadcasts his love to work the redemption of the would-be victims of such situations.

What is more, God does not reveal his love for these alone. He is also working for the redemption of the people "who, because of their upbringing, see a picture of racial differences in which the details of the present obscure the possibilities of the future." [12] This being so, we must not allow our own sympathy for the underdog to blind us to God's concern for the people who do not share it. No matter how bigoted the people who have thus far spurned the imitation of God's attitude toward their fellows, they too are God's creatures; they too are candidates for redemption; they too are the objects of God's love. Here we do well to recall our Lord's parable of the loving Father (Luke 15:11-32). For if he does not hesitate to welcome the repentant prodigal back home, neither does he jump to chase the unrepentant prodigal from home. This father's love embraces the smug bigot as well as the wandering profligate. Such is the love of our "Father which is in heaven," the one whom the Bible calls us to imitate.

Summary

The biblical writers see man as a creature of dignity, and they treat him accordingly. They see men as equals, not because the achievements of some do not dwarf those of others, but because all men are equally dependent on God for the gift of life and a sphere in which to order it. They see each generation as God's opportunity for a new start, not because all generations are equally good or bad, but because God so controls history as to reconcile divine sovereignty and human freedom. They emphasize the social dimension of human nature, not because of any lack of appreciation for man as an individual, but in recognition of the pervasive influence of the life of man on men. They invite men to the imitation of God's attitude toward their neighbors, not from the belief that they will be able to build Utopia if they accept this invitation, but in the conviction that they will plunge both themselves and their neighbors into hell if they do not.

CHAPTER IX

The Identity and Mission of the "Chosen People"

THE TYPICAL BIBLICAL DEFENSE OF SEGREGATION BEGINS AND ENDS with the idea of chosen peoples. It stems from the notion that God has selected certain specific peoples for the occupation of certain specific places through the whole sweep of human history. It even traces national and racial boundaries to an act of God at the very dawn of civilization.

Most of the people who champion segregation on biblical grounds content themselves with a singular version of the above argument. That is, instead of contending for the idea of chosen peoples, they contend only for "the idea of a 'chosen people.'" [1] A corresponding change normally accompanies this shift in number. Instead of turning to the Bible in search of proof texts for their case, they seek from it only some precedent in the history of God's people for their exclusivist attitudes and practices. And this, with a minimum of difficulty, they manage to find. Indeed, some of them have already evolved from the biblical doctrine of the chosen people a three-pronged defense of their position. It features the following propositions: (1) If Israel had not been superior to other peoples, God would not have chosen Israel to be his people; (2) since God's kingdom is not of this world, his people should spend their time getting ready for the next; (3) in view of the exclusion of the great masses of men by divine choice, the chosen bear no special responsibility for the excluded.

Needless to add, the people who argue these propositions do

not hesitate to put themselves in the place of the chosen people, be they Israel after the flesh, Israel after the faith, or, in keeping with the New Testament view, the Israel of God. But do these propositions represent legitimate inferences from the biblical view of the people of God?

The Choice of God

Numerous members of the covenant community interpreted their unique relationship to God as a guarantee of special privileges and immunities. Some Israelites drew from it support for their belief in the necessary survival of Israel as a political entity. Many treated it as evidence for their belief in the inviolability of the temple. Others used it as an explanation of their assurance of an economic boom. Still others hauled it into court to justify their anticipation of continued good health and a long, happy life. What is more, despite the numerous changes which followed hard on the heels of the break of the Israel of the Old Testament with the Israel of the New Testament, certain members of the Israel of God perpetuated this tradition. For example, some of the Thessalonians even turned their membership in the elect community into an excuse for cessation from labor. If God's people, why work just to eat? Why not eat without working?

Both Testaments introduce us to people who interpreted their peculiar relationship to God as warrant for the assumption of special privileges without corresponding responsibilities. The wide prevalence of this assumption throughout the biblical period lies beyond question. Indeed, there's only one other fact about the biblical view of the people of God of which we can be more certain. And this is the readiness of the more nearly normative writers of the Bible to relegate this concept of the chosen people to the periphery.[2] Indeed, they attack it as a rank perversion of the biblical notion of the chosen people. Typical illustrations of this attitude appear in the Old Testament account of the birth of Israel [3] and the Pauline idea of justification by grace.[4]

One day while tending the flock of Jethro on the slopes of Sinai, the mountain of God, Moses receives the revelation of God's purpose to use him in the deliverance of Israel from Egyptian bondage. This revelation provides Moses with the dynamic for his inspiring performance in the lead role of the Exodus drama. Close in the wake of this transforming experience, now a man with a mission, Moses returns to Egypt as the agent of God in Israel's deliverance.

Lest his plan be mistaken as a mere bid for political freedom, he grounds his plea for Israelite unity in recognition of Yahweh as the God of Israel and Israel as the people of Yahweh. The acceptance of this invitation brings in its train a sudden increase in popular agitation for release from the yoke of Pharaoh. Smoldering resentment bursts into flaming rebellion. Prostrate Israel arises in defiance of mighty Egypt (Exod. 13). But the Egyptians do not drop dead at the sight of opposition. They take after the fleeing Israelites. However, the escapees from Egypt receive aid from an unexpected source. Some kind of natural calamity plunges large numbers of the pursuing Egyptians to an unexpected death (Exod. 14:26-31).

The Israelites do not wonder very long about the source of their help. They cannot explain their remarkable deliverance as anything short of an act of divine intervention in their behalf (Exod. 15:1). They interpret their escape as God's confirmation of the promise made Israel through Moses.

Following their escape from the clutches of the Egyptians, the Israelites remain in the wilderness for the celebration of a festival to Yahweh. They call this feast, still observed by the Jews, the Passover. While this observance may conceivably antedate the Exodus, from this time forth the ritual for the celebration of this festival serves as a solemn reminder of the divine act of redemption associated with the Exodus. "And when . . . your son asks you, 'What does this mean?' you shall say to him, 'By strength of hand the Lord brought us out of Egypt, from the house of bondage.' " (Exod. 13:14 R.S.V.)

This deliverance marks the birth of the Israelite claim to a special relationship with God. One distinction marks this claim above all others—the complete absence of any rational basis for it. The Israelites look beyond both Moses and themselves for the explanation of their deliverance from Pharaoh's army. They do not become the people of God because they choose Yahweh to be the God of Israel. They become the people of God because Yahweh chooses Israel to be his people. In short, just as they interpret the Exodus as an act of divine intervention by a merciful God, so they trace the appearance of Israel as a peculiar people to the choice of that same merciful God, the creator and the redeemer of the world, the lord and the judge of history.

The biblical version of the Exodus has long been a source of embarrassment to ethical idealists. Why do the biblical writers, they ask, bypass the character of the people in search of the explanation of the Exodus? Why do they not give the Israelites at last some of the credit for the event to which Israel traces her beginning as the people of God?

Paul's substitution of the Israel of God for Israel after the flesh marks only one of several significant shifts in what can only be described as a theological revolution. Two of these changes deserve our special attention. They seem to be based in presuppositions more congenial to ethical idealists. First of all,

Paul's interest in salvation begins and, we could probably add, ends with deliverance from sin. Then, in accordance with this transformation of the whole idea of salvation, he throws open the doors of the church "to all human beings from the mere fact that they are human beings." [5] Having thus made redemption equally open to all, irrespective of race, sex or previous condition of servitude, it would seem that the moral determinists can now relax. How can Paul keep from making membership in the church, the outward and visible sign of inclusion among the redeemed, to hinge on human merit? How else can he interpret membership in the Israel of God if not as the reaction of God to the action of man? Paul's answer to this question comes as a bitter disappointment to the prematurely elated moral determinists, for Paul does not interpret salvation as the reaction of God to the action of man. He sees salvation, instead, as the reaction of man to the action of God. Israel's great prophets could not conceive of Israel's deliverance from Egypt apart from the prevenient grace of God. Similarly, Paul cannot conceive of man's deliverance from sin apart from the prevenient grace of God.

The chosen people have no ground for boasting of their deliverance, either from Egypt or from sin. In both instances, according to the normative writers of both Testaments, they owe their status to the mercy of God. They cannot trace it to their own volition. This being the case, the following words could just as well be a prophet's words to the Israel of Ahab or Josiah as those of a New Testament writer to the Israel of God: "For by grace are ye saved through faith; and that not of yourselves: it is the gift of God: not of works, lest any man should boast" (Eph. 2:8-9).

But members of the holy community, old and new, do boast. They ignore prophetic and apostolic warnings against the temptation to trace their special status to their own superiority. They fall victim to it, generation after generation. Even though they may not originally have been superior to other people, they now feel that they are—if for no other reason than their occupation of the holy land, worship in the temple, descent from Abraham, obedience to the law of Moses, or membership in the church of Jesus Christ!

As often, however, as the chosen people begin thus to find in their land, their law, their lineage, their worship, their residence, or, for that matter, anything else of theirs, any basis whatever for special treatment at the hands of God, the biblical writers snatch it from them. And with a solemn reminder of the threatening dissolution of the covenant between them and their God. Not only do they tell them that they have only whatever value, importance, and dignity God has conferred upon them. They also tell them that as soon as they cease to acknowledge this fact they will lose that dignity, importance, and value. Any attempt to justify God's choice by reference to the character of those chosen voids that choice. Therefore, if the people of God want to know why God chose them, they had better look to the character of the choosing God for their answer. And they had better not look elsewhere. They had better be especially careful not to seek it in their own character. Indeed, they cannot look for it here very long without jeopardizing their very status as the chosen people, without provoking God to raise up a prophet to say to them, as once he moved Hosea to say to them: "Ye are not my people, and I will not be your God" (1:9).

Will we, like disobedient Israel, imagine that God has chosen us, if at all, because of what we are or do or have? Dare we claim his call because, as privileged whites and democracy-loving Christians, we can bring to his service a better education, greater political power, and more social influence than any other people? If so, we do well to recall two facts about the biblical view of the chosen people: (1) God, and not man, does the choosing; (2) God does the choosing on his, and not man's, terms. We have already commented in some detail on the first of these observations. We shall not do the same for the second, however. Since nobody could possibly improve on what Paul has to say in this connection, we shall leave this point with the following quotation from his letter to the Christians at Corinth:

God hath chosen the foolish things of the world to confound the wise; and . . . the weak things of the world to confound the things which are mighty; and base things of the world, and things which are despised. . . , yea, and things which are not, to bring to nought things that are: that no flesh should glory in his presence. (I Cor. 1:27-29.)

If God cannot accept wisdom, strength, dignity or, yea, even existence as a legitimate ground for pride in his presence, dare we believe that he will sanction the treatment of race as a reason to "glory in his presence"?

A New Community in History

Many American Christians tended for a long time to look on the people of God as a collection of unattached saints.[6] What God's people had in common, they felt, began and ended with the special relationship each bore to God. And this, quite often, carried with it no demand for the achievement of a new relationship of redeemed men in the "common life in the Church." Christians should not join the battle for integration, a spokesman of this view declared, because "Christ's kingdom is not of this world." [7]

144

Today, however, you could almost spot the second-rate theologian by his readiness to defend this view. One of the most remarkable facts of our time is the wholesale rejection of this idea by all the really top theologians of Christendom.[8] And yet it's not so remarkable either. Considering the rediscovery in our time of biblical theology, this development was really inevitable. We could never really have rediscovered the basic message of the Bible without simultaneously recovering a new and deep appreciation for the people of God as a *people*, both in history and beyond history.[9] The Bible never treats the chosen people as a sort of disembodied soul. It sees them rather as members of a spiritual organism: as members of an organism who can never thrive in detachment—from God, from history, or from one another.

Since the Old Testament only rarely hints at any sort of afterlife, we need take only a brief look at its demonstration of the truth of the above proposition. Old Testament writers seem to feel that if God's people do not manifest the fruits of their relationship in this life and this world, they will never do so. If they do not undertake the organization of the historical community of Israel on the basis of the divine character, then they must abandon all hope for the appearance of such a community, ever. It's quite clearly a case of now or never. Just as clearly, at least in the case of the overwhelming majority of them, they refuse to let it be a case of never.

Certainly the prophets of Israel make no allowances for the perpetuation of evil, public or private, in the life of Israel. On the sole condition of repentance, of which they assume everybody to be capable, their words of promise hail the appearance of a new reality. *And in the here and now of this world!* They foresee a reality "which includes in a new creation the individual

145

as well as the people, the nations as well as the whole of nature, and . . . resolves the insuperable resistance to a life bound by an absolute obligation to God's will." [10]

The priestly writers of the Old Testament take an additional, if somewhat misguided, step in quest of even closer co-operation with the divine will in human society. They codify God's will. They reduce the moral norm to a readily ascertainable system. Thus they define the means of establishing and maintaining harmony between God and man on earth.

Only in one instance does the Old Testament express a clear-cut belief in a glorious resurrection (Daniel). Then what we get may best be described as the mere extension of the prophetic-priestly concern for the renewal of life in this world. The life of the resurrected has this earth as its scene.[11] Moreover, as in prophetic thought, conformity with the divine will continues to be the indispensable prerequisite for the enjoyment of fellowship with God.[12]

The Old Testament writers manifest little interest in the world to come—and even less in the hope of a glorious future life. Their central theme turns on the demand for the transformation of this present life in keeping with the divine character. By the same token, when men ignore or compromise this demand, as they inevitably do, the prophets do not attribute this defection to an ancient curse. They trace it to an act of disobedience by those on whom the curse falls.

The problem here stems from the interpretation of the New Testament hope of a glorious future for God's people as an excuse for the disregard of the here and now. But is this an accurate interpretation? Does the New Testament drown its concern for the relationship of the redeemed in this world in gleeful anticipation of their occupation of the next? Does it ignore the church militant because of a one-sided concern for the church triumphant? Does it reduce the present demands on God's people out of deference for their approaching occupation of the world to come?

All these questions must be answered with a firm negative. Indeed the New Testament demands the witness of the Christian community to the "form of life." [13] expected of the world to come, because *the world to come is already here.* Amos Wilder, commenting on the reference among Gentile Christians to Jesus as Lord, Son of God, and Saviour, writes:

When such titles were given to Augustus, for example, they expressed the homage of the Empire to one who had ushered in a new world of peace and concord throughout the entire civilized world, putting an end to the bloody period of civil war and anarchy. Jesus receives these same titles, *and the analogy is not confined to titles* [italics mine].[14]

The New Testament everywhere assumes the relevance of Christ's redemptive work to the life of this age and this world. Though it wisely betrays a very cautious attitude about the possibility of achieving moral perfection in this life, it nevertheless treats "the atonement . . . as a finished work." [15] Hunter notes:

For all the first Christians, the New Age has come "with power" in the death, resurrection, and exaltation of Jesus the Messiah. With this great event the period of the law is over; the Spirit has come; the *ecclesia* [church] of God is a reality; righteousness is a *fait accompli*; and Christians are "sons of God" enjoying here and now a foretaste—a first instalment—of the glorious inheritance that God has promised to them that love him.[16]

If now we ask, Does the New Testament include deliverance

from the curse of the Fall in its description of the atoning work? we have only to look at a few of the chief elements in Paul's doctrine of the church. Two of Paul's terms for the church call for special consideration. The first is "the body of Christ." The rabbinic view of the unity of mankind in Adam greatly illuminates the meaning of this phrase. The rabbis describe the body of Adam as a sort of corporation in which all members of the old humanity hold membership. One passage even discusses this unity in terms of the attachment of all men to different parts of Adam's body: one man clings to a lock of hair, another to an ear, or another to a finger. Two aims underlie the rabbinic usage of this figure. One is to bring men to the recognition of their oneness in virtue of the descent of all mankind from a common progenitor. The other is to lend force to the appeal for the recognition of human equality and the practice of social justice.[17]

The relevance of all this to Paul's doctrine of the church becomes clear once we recall the apostle's description of Christ as the Second Adam. As he speaks of Christ, the Second Adam, as the head of the church, we may likewise speak of the church as "the body of Christ" or "the body of the Second Adam." By the same token, if membership in the body of the first Adam implies the unity and equality of the old humanity, then membership in the body of the Second Adam can hardly imply less of the new humanity. That is to say, "a new corporate personality is created in Christ," the Second Adam, in which all members of the redeemed community have union with God in Christ and with one another.[18]

The federal view of man holds the key to Paul's interpretation of the work of the two Adams. Paul sees mankind as a corporation whose members participate in the actions, and the effects of the actions, of their representatives. Both Adam and Christ thus involve all mankind in their work as representative heads of the corporation of humanity. Adam, in his role as the representative of this body, plunged all mankind into liability to sin. By bequeathing to all subsequent men a corrupted flesh, he rendered them vulnerable to the powers of evil, which Paul calls "the elemental spirits of the universe." [19] Through the inheritance of this weakened body of flesh, all men participate in the consequences of the sin of the first Adam—or they did until the appearance of Jesus Christ.

Christ, in his role as the representative man, won a victory over these hostile powers for all the members of the human corporation. Because he shared with us sinful men our fleshly weakness, we can share with him his victory over this fleshly weakness. Because he partook of our sin-tainted humanity, we can partake of his sin-free humanity. Because he bore "the image of the man of dust," we can bear "the image of the man of heaven" (I Cor. 15:49 R.S.V.). Because he became one with us in our vulnerability to the effects of the Fall, we can become one with him in his immunity to the effects of the Fall. Christ became one with us in the assumption of the liabilities to which the human corporation fell heir as the result of the sinful work of the first Adam. And because he did, we can become one with him in the assumption of the benefits to which the human corporation fell heir as the result of his redemptive work as the Second Adam. Just as the disobedience of the first Adam closes the door on the filial relation between God and man intended by the creator, so the obedience of the Second Adam paves the way for the recovery of this relation.

Paul's description in Romans of men who receive the benefits of the work of the Second Adam clearly indicates the relevance of Christ's redemptive work to this life and this world. Certainly the apostle gives slight encouragement to those who postpone the appropriation of such benefits until some future consummation. Men "in Christ" have already been delivered from "the spirit of bondage" (8:15). They walk, not "after the flesh, but after the Spirit" (8:4). "Therefore, brethren, we are debtors, not to the flesh, to live after the flesh" (8:12). Because Christ has redeemed us from the spirit of bondage, we no longer have reason to live in fear; "for . . . neither death, *nor life*, nor angels, nor principalities, nor powers, *nor things present*[!], nor things *to come . . . shall be able to separate us from the love of God, which is in Christ Jesus our Lord*" (8:38-39).

But the real clincher for Paul's belief in the Second Adam's cancellation of the effects of the sin of the first Adam comes in his reference to men "in Christ" as members of a "new creation." Rabbinic Judaism sometimes employed this term in its description of the life of the messianic age. Since the rabbis anticipated the restoration of the conditions of the original creation at the dawn of the messianic era, they referred to it as the "new creation." Here the difference between them and Paul is only one of tense. Whereas they look forward to the dawn of the messianic era, Paul looks back on the dawn of the messianic era. Whereas they await the appearance of the "new creation," Paul celebrates its arrival. By the same token, whereas they still await deliverance from the effects of the fall of the first Adam, Paul treats it as an accomplished fact.

Thus Paul's deep concern for manifestation in the here and now of the oneness of the redeemed community becomes clear in his use of the body as an analogy for the relationship that should obtain among the various members of Christ's body (I Cor. 12; cf. Rom. 12:4-6). Just as the malfunctioning of any member of the human body has a debilitating effect on all its other members, even so does the malfunctioning of any member of the church affect the body of Christ. Just as in the former each member serves its own peculiar and indispensable function, so also in the latter; as in the former the different members honor each the others, not despite, but because of a variety of gifts or functions, so should they also in the latter. In both bodies all the various members stand in a complementary and interdependent relation one with the others, and they must achieve their destiny —if at all!—in unqualified and complete co-operation. This means there's no room in the body of Christ for the prima donna. Since the malfunctioning of any organ of the human body can impair the functioning of the whole, what right has the hand to lord it over the foot? Who can make sense of such discrimination? Paul would deny that anybody could. Similarly, Paul would deny the possibility of ever justifying the practice of invidious discrimination by the members of Christ's body. Does this mean the more fortunate members of the church must bear the burdens of the underprivileged members of the Christian fellowship? Here is Paul's answer:

For the body is not one member, but many. If the foot shall say, Because I am not the hand, I am not of the body; is it therefore not of the body? And if the ear shall say, Because I am not the eye, I am not of the body; is it therefore not of the body? If the whole body were an eye, where were the hearing? If the whole were hearing, where were the smelling? But now hath God set the members every one of them in the body, as it hath pleased him. And if they were all one member, where were the body? But now are they many members, yet but one body. And the eye cannot say unto the hand, I have no need of thee: nor again the head to the feet, I have no need of you. Nay, much more those members of the body, which seem to be more feeble, are necessary: and those members of the body, which we think to be less honourable, upon these we bestow more abundant honour; and our uncomely parts have more abundant comeliness. For our comely parts have no need: but God hath tempered the body together, having given more abundant honour to that part which lacked: That there should be no schism in the body; but that the members should have the same care one for another. And whether one member suffer, all the members suffer with it; or one member be honoured, all the members rejoice with it. Now ye are the body of Christ, and members in particular. (I Cor. 12:14-27.)

So much for the impossibility of enlisting Paul's support for the interpretation of the Christian life and fellowship as a vague, suprahistorical, mystical union of the believer with his Lord. We simply cannot question Paul's concern for the manifestation in history of the new relationship Christians have in Christ with one another.

Now for another question. Just how far must this relationship penetrate the common life? Far enough to touch economic and cultural tensions?

Consideration of this question calls for a look at another of Paul's favorite words, *koinonia*, a term he often employed in referring to the church. Scholars have often translated this word as "fellowship." Because this rendering has strengthened the temptation of our contemporaries to think of the church in vague and vaporous terms, we shall employ the original. *Koinonia* carried with it from contemporary everyday Greek a quite substantial, if somewhat varied, meaning into the New Testament. In secular parlance it could refer to the reciprocal relation of business partners, the acknowledgment of mutual responsibilities within the marriage relation or the personal relation of a man to his Maker.[20] Paul's description of the church as the *koinonia* of believers seems to presuppose a combination of all three meanings. At least one thing is certain. He offers little encouragement to the pious folk who, though glad enough to share a common Lord, faith, and baptism with the underprivileged, will not support their bid for a square deal on Commerce Street. Membership in the *koinonia* of Christians carries with it a responsibility for the welfare, physical as well as spiritual, of the other members of Christ's body. Indeed, Paul almost makes the manifestation of such concern a test of the genuineness of the Christian community. On three different occasions he refers to this community as a *koinonia* in support of his plea for a generous offering for the oppressed Christians of the Jerusalem Church (Rom. 15:26; II Cor. 8:4; 9:13). Especially instructive are his words to the Christians in Rome:

> But now I go unto Jerusalem to minister unto the saints. For it hath pleased them of Macedonia and Achaia to make a certain contribution for the poor saints which are at Jerusalem. It hath pleased them verily; and their debtors they are. For if the Gentiles have been made partakers of their spiritual things, their duty is also to minister unto them in carnal things. (Rom. 15:25-27.)

Paul's use of the term *koinonia* to describe the life of the Christian community suggests the repudiation of the people who so define religion as to exclude the battle for bread from its concerns. Paul interprets the Christian *koinonia* in terms consistent with his Hebraic view of man. Because he sees man as an irreducible compound of body and soul, he defines the responsibility of the *koinonia* in appropriately broad and inclusive terms. If genuinely Christian, it will manifest itself in complete concern for the welfare of the whole man in his total existence. This means the inclusion of every single dimension of man's life—physical, economic, cultural, social and spiritual. We may even wonder if Paul did not deliberately employ this term as a sort of reminder of the seriousness with which he wants us to take his description of the church as a body.

Beyond all doubt, Paul's view of the church calls for the manifestation of the new relationship which Christians bear to one another on the plane of history and in the realm of economics. We have only one further question to ask. Does he call for the disregard of such racial differences as we know in Christendom today in the manifestation of this concern? Since the church in Paul's day seems to have been largely confined to people of the same race, we cannot say. We can only recall our earlier findings of what he did with the nearest approximation in the life of the primitive church, the question of the relation between Christians of Gentile background and those of Jewish background, to a race problem. He faced it head on and he resolved it without delay. Then, in season and out, he sought for the incorporation of this solution into the everyday life of the Christian community. Regardless of background, whether Jewish or Gentile, when men and women come together as members of the *koinonia* of Christ, he seems to have felt, they will bring their blessings with them. It matters not whether they be spiritual, as in the case of the Jews, or material, as in the case of the Gentiles. They will bring these blessings with them into the Christian community. Then, without hesitation or invidious discrimination, they will make them available to fellow Christians according to need.

Paul did not face a race problem. But he faced a cultural cleavage every whit as emotionally charged and, hence, as potentially explosive as our race problem. And what did he do? He proclaimed a supracultural gospel for a supracultural church.

154

What is more, he pleaded for evidence of the conquest of this prejudice in the common life of the Christian community. What if, instead of a cleavage of cultures, Paul had faced a cleavage of races? Would he not have been just as vigorous in the proclamation of a supraracial gospel for a supraracial church? And would he not have pressed just as earnestly for evidence of the conquest of this prejudice?

The Vocation of the Chosen People

The people who interpret their election by God as an excuse for inaction, as Christians who deny any religious basis for social action have so often done, do so without biblical support. The biblical writers, almost without exception, denounce this static notion. They come out, instead, for a dynamic version of the identity and mission of the people of God. If God's people would not lose their identity, they give us to understand, they must fulfill the mission for whose performance they were chosen. And this mission has two references too; one within, the other without. Not only must the members of this community run ahead of themselves to stay within it. They must share it with the outs in order to remain among the ins.[21]

If now we ask, How does the New Testament conceive the vocation of the church as regards the first aspect of this mission? the answer is that of setting "the example for what human relationships are meant to be." [22] Paul provides us with the clearest biblical warrant for this assertion in his presentation of the church as the body of Christ. That is, provided we interpret this figure against the background of the New Testament references to Christ as "the head of the church" (Eph. 5:23; Col. 1:18; cf. also such passages as I Cor. 3:23 and 11:3, which clearly imply just the kind of relation of Christians to

155

Christ as suggested in these figures). These two figures together, and this is how we must interpret them, imply just such a relationship between Christ and Christians as exists between a man's head and body. The various members of the body of man act at the direction of the head of man. Just so, the various members of the body of Christ should act at the direction of the head of the church. Each member should be able to say of himself, with Paul, "Christ liveth in me" (Gal. 2:20).

This concept implies a sharp qualification of the effort to extend the democratic principle to the church. We do not elect Christ as head of the church; quite the contrary, Christ, as the head of the church, elects us to membership in his body. Christ's headship of the church does not hinge on our exercise of the free ballot. Yet our membership in his body does hinge on the nature of our response to his directions. If we treat them as the edicts of a sovereign, well and good; if not, then how great the cost—to the health of the offending member, to the witness of the weakened body, and to the cause of a righteous and loving head.

This facet of biblical thought contains some rather valuable suggestions as to the questions with which churchmen should approach the problems of race. For example, here are a few of the questions which would seem to be ruled out by this consideration: What will happen to our budget if we begin admitting nonwhites into our predominantly white churches, or vice versa? Can we afford to lose the members such a policy would alienate? Would my endorsement of it, as minister, precipitate a widespread clamor for my resignation?

If Christ be the head of the church, then such questions can hardly serve as a fit point of departure for the discussion of racial tensions. Indeed, if Christ be head of the church, there's only one place to begin the discussion of this or, for that matter, any other problem. That's with the question, attributed to Paul in some versions of the New Testament: "Lord, what wilt thou have me [us] to do?" (Acts 9:6).

The Bible characteristically and consistently demands from God's people an example of God-directed life in community. But this duty is not what the New Testament regards as the primary task of the church. "That essential task is to witness to Jesus Christ and make known what God has done through Him, in order that more and more people may come to Christian faith and find their loyal place in the worship and the fellowship of the church. The basic task was evangelistic and missionary." [23] It was to make ins of the outs.

If now we ask, Which ones? we must turn to Acts for our answer. Actually, however, this story of developing Christianity does not yield an answer; it yields several answers. Or to put it more accurately, it suggests the several steps on the way to the particular answer with which the church finally resolved the matter. For if it betrays the church's reluctance to launch a world-wide movement, it does not fail simultaneously to indicate steady and consistent progress toward the evolution of an ecumenical concept of her mission. This trend begins with the admission of proselyte Jews on the same basis as Jews from birth (6:5). It gathers additional momentum with the decision to welcome Samaritans on an equal footing with Jews (8:5-6). A subsequent decision in favor of the admission of God-fearers (11:18), Gentiles who observed some of the practices of Judaism, left the church with only one major obstacle still to hurdle in its bid for recognition as a truly universal faith, the admission of Gentiles who did not observe the law. But the church leaped this obstacle, as we have seen, in what may be regarded as one of the most difficult and decisive forward steps in Christian history. After a long and heated debate of the grounds for the admission of Gentiles with no previous connection with Judaism, the church decided not to demand from such converts subjection to the more esoteric and ceremonial features of the law of Moses (Acts 15; cf. Gal. 2:1-10).[24]

This decision marks the turning point in the debate over the scope of the gospel. The later writers of the New Testament scarcely bother even to discuss this issue—and for good reason. They do not treat the view that the gospel is for all the people throughout all the world as a question for an ecclesiastical debate. They treat it as a presupposition of Christian action. And they act accordingly. They cut the cloth of the missionary enterprise of the church on the pattern of an ecumenical view of the gospel. If God in Christ would extend to all men the benefits of his atoning love, they could find no basis for the exclusion of any man from the church's witness to that love. At any rate, this assumption clearly underlies the more explicit formulations of their view of the church's task.

And this gospel of the kingdom shall be preached in *all the world for a witness unto all nations.* (Matt. 24:14.)

Go ye therefore, and *teach all nations*, baptizing them in the name of the Father, and of the Son, and of the Holy Ghost. (Matt. 28:19.)

For God so loved *the world*, that he gave his only begotten Son, that whosoever believeth in him should not perish, but have everlasting life. For God sent . . . his Son into the world . . . that the world through him might be saved. (John 3:16-17.)

But ye shall receive power, after that the Holy Ghost is come upon you: and ye shall be witnesses unto me both in Jerusalem, and in

all Judaea, and in Samaria, and unto *the uttermost part of the earth.*
(Acts 1:8.)

These New Testament statements of our Christian mission
clearly identify, at least by implication, the church's chief task
as a double responsibility. The first lays upon it the task of bearing the invitation of God in Christ to participation in a fellowship in which all have equal rights "on the simple basis of
repentance, faith, and Spirit-led living." [25] The other calls for
the demonstration of a quality of life that will incline men
toward a favorable response to this invitation. Since she cannot
share what she does not have, the church must be, at least in
some measure, what she asks the world to become.

This demand for at least a measure of consistency between the
gospel we proclaim and the life we reveal raises some disturbing
questions for us all. And especially for those of us who have
been inclined to feel that we should not try to solve the race
problem among Christians until after we have converted all the
heathen to Christianity. For how can we expect non-Christians
to heed the proclamation of a gospel for all races by a racially
divided church? So long as we work with non-Christian members
of our own race for the exclusion from our fellowship of Christians of other races, how can we expect the serious consideration
of the church's claim to be, though "elect from every nation, . . .
one o'er all the earth"? So long as we allow racial barriers to
divide us "in Christ," do we not in so doing cancel out our plea
to non-Christians for the recognition of Christ as the answer
to the problem of race? Why should we be surprised at the
world's disregard of the proclamation of an all-inclusive gospel
by a less than all-inclusive church? In short, if the gospel of
redemptive love has not transformed the lives and the relation-

ships of the men who bear it, why should we be surprised if the men who hear it do not heed it?

Summary

The biblical doctrine of the chosen people offers only negligible, if any, support to the champions of a separatist claim. Indeed, if we limit our consideration to those biblical writers whose view of the identity and mission of the chosen people can be reconciled with the New Testament's most fully developed view of the church, we can put the matter even more emphatically. These writers perforate every single one of the propositions, one by one, which the separatists have allegedly deduced from the Bible in support of an exclusive gospel for a privileged few.

These writers trace the origin of the people of God to the choice, not of the chosen people, but of the choosing God. As a consequence, they do not view membership in the holy community as a ground for boasting; they do not give man credit for the work of God. Indeed, unlike the separatists, they look on the chosen people's special status before God as more a source of agony and humility than of joy and boasting. They see this choice, not as an excuse to play the role of strutting sovereign among suffering servants, but as the call of God to become a suffering servant among strutting sovereigns. They see it, not as a privilege to parade, but as a responsibility to carry. "Every one to whom much is given," Jesus of Nazareth declared, "of him will much be required" (Luke 12:48 R.S.V.).

These writers do not treat the hope of the chosen people for a glorious future as an excuse for the uncritical acceptance of injustice in the here and now. They hail the hope of heaven, not as an excuse for the denial of justice and equality among

160

men, but as a motive for labor in pursuit of justice and equality among men. And justice, as viewed in the Bible, does not end with the demand that we do as we are done by. It also means the refusal to claim for ourselves what we are unwilling to grant unto others. To put it briefly, they expect us to do better by the Lord's prayer than turn into hollow mockery this petition: "Thy will be done in earth, as it is in heaven." [26]

These writers look on the chosen people, not primarily as a saved people, but as a saving people. They see them as members of a fellowship with a task. And what is this task? That of fashioning for Jesus Christ, the author of an ecumenical gospel for an ecumenical church, a body fit for his habitation.

NOTES

PART I

Introduction

1. Article in *The Nashville Banner*, June 5, 1954.
2. Article in *The Nashville Tennessean*, March 11, 1956.
3. Ch. I, sec. 10.
4. From the address "Segregation and Bible Teachings."
5. *A Christian View on Segregation* (Winona, Miss.: Association of Citizens' Councils, 1954), p. 8.

Chapter 1. The Key Passages from the Book of Genesis

1. See C. W. Howell's booklet *Segregation* (Columbia, Tenn.: n.p., n.d.), p. 5, in which he asserts: "God has separated or segregated the sons of Adam, and has determined the bounds and limits of their settlements."
2. See statement attributed in a news item to E. K. Oldham by *The Citizens' Council* (Jackson, Miss.), May, 1956.
3. *Op. cit.*, p. 9.
4. *An Encyclopedia of World History*, ed. William L. Langer (Boston: Houghton Mifflin Co., 1947), p. 12.
5. As a matter of fact, we are told in *Ibid.*: "Thus . . . pure racial types cannot . . . be said to exist. . . . For this reason attempted classifications of races differ widely and the lack of a standard nomenclature is the cause of much confusion."
6. A. H. Sayce, *The Races of the Old Testament* (Oxford, Eng.: The Religious Tract Society, 1891), pp. 41-42, wrote toward the close of the last century: "Attempts have been made to explain the names of the three sons of Noah as referring to the colour of the skin. Japheth has been compared with the Assyrian *ippatu* 'white,' Shem with the Assyrian *samu* 'olive-coloured,' while in Ham etymologists have seen the Hebrew *kham* 'to be hot.' But all such attempts are of very doubtful value. It is, for instance, a long stride from the meaning of 'heat' to that of 'blackness'—a meaning, indeed, which the Hebrew word never bears." This view still holds the field, as suggested by Edmund D. Soper, *Racism: A World Issue* (Nashville: Abingdon Press, 1947), p. 35.
7. Sayce, *op. cit.*, p. 40.
8. See Gillespie, *op. cit.*, p. 9, for a typical suggestion of this point. Less informed men, undisturbed by the obvious textual obstacles to this argument, exhibit much less restraint in their use of this passage.

9. George Rawlinson, *Five Great Monarchies* (New York: Dodd, Mead & Co., 1881), pp. 75-76.

10. I. vi. 2.

11. "The Old Testament World," *The Interpreter's Bible*, I, 238.

12. So Gillespie, *op. cit.*, p. 9.

13. *Ibid.*

14. "Genesis," *Peake's Commentary on the Bible*, ed. A. S. Peake (New York: Thomas Nelson & Sons, 1920), p. 145.

Chapter 2. The Demands for Racial Purity

1. *Op. cit.*, p. 10.

2. See II Sam. 18:9; I Kings 1:33; 18:5.

3. Ethel J. Alpenfels, in support of the "hybrid vigor" theory, *Sense and Nonsense about Race* (New York: Friendship Press, 1957), pp. 49-50, notes: "There are twenty-nine studies that have been made on racial mixtures . . . and in each case the children tend to be taller, smarter, and otherwise superior to their parents." One would be hard put to it on the basis of biblical genealogies to challenge this view—even on moral and spiritual grounds.

4. See Bernhard W. Anderson, *Understanding the Old Testament* (New York: Prentice-Hall, 1957), pp. 96 ff.

5. For a sympathetic yet critical evaluation of Ezra's work, see John Bright, *The Kingdom of God* (Nashville: Abingdon Press, 1953), pp. 172-76.

6. Whom Louis Finkelstein, "Ezra," *An Encyclopedia of Religion*, p. 269, hails as the founder of rabbinic legalism.

Chapter 3. The Scope of Christian Love

1. News item in the publication of *The Association of Citizens' Councils of South Carolina* (Summerton, S. C.), no date.

2. Rogers answers the question, Why this defection of modern ministers? with the charge of "socialism." Preachers of former times, unaffected by this pressure, had full knowledge of the above New Testament distinction. "The ministers to our forefathers had the Bible," he declares, "but not Socialism; and for them segregation was compatible with Christianity. The only difference is Socialism. The Bible hasn't changed; and if Socialism is omitted, segregation and Christianity are still compatible." If Rogers were as up on American history as he is down on today's preachers, he would scarcely have denied the existence of socialism in the days of his forefathers. At any rate, one of the most eloquent and learned defenders of slavery in the 1840's, James Henly Thornwell, traced the fever for abolition to the activity, among others, of socialists. He declared: "The parties in this conflict are not merely abolitionists, and Slaveholders; they are Atheists, Socialists, Communists, Red Republicans, Jacobians on the one side, and the friends of order and regulated freedom on the other." *The Collected Writings of J. H. Thornwell*, IV, ed. J. B. Adger and J. L. Girardeau (Richmond: Presbyterian Committee of Publication, 1873), pp. 405-6. Unless "the great

and learned churchmen in the days of our forefathers" were as ignorant of current events as Rogers would have us believe modern preachers are of New Testament Greek, our forefathers were not so unfamiliar with socialism as he would have us think!

3. *Op. cit.*

4. Ethelbert Stauffer, "*agapaō, agapē, agapētos,*" *Theologisches Wörterbuch zum Neuen Testament,* Erster Band, I, 36.

5. *Agape and Eros,* tr. Philip S. Watson (Philadelphia: The Westminster Press, 1953), pp. 61-74.

6. *Ibid.,* pp. 75-76.

7. For a brilliant interpretation of Christian ethics in the light of this presupposition, see Paul Ramsey, *Basic Christian Ethics* (New York: Charles Scribner's Sons, 1950).

8. Article in *The Nashville Tennessean,* March 11, 1956.

9. See Ernst Troeltsch, *The Social Teaching of the Christian Churches,* I (New York: The Macmillan Co., 1950), 80 ff., who says the early Christians began their invasion of the Roman Empire with the feeling that they must "respect the existing regime and . . . turn it to good account, since their citizenship is not on earth but in Heaven."

10. *An Outline of Biblical Theology* (Philadelphia: The Westminster Press, 1946), p. 310.

11. *The State in the New Testament* (New York: Charles Scribner's Sons, 1956), p. 4.

12. *Ibid.,* pp. 90-91.

13. *Ibid.,* pp. 71-85.

14. So Liston Pope, *The Kingdom Beyond Caste* (New York: The Friendship Press, 1957), p. 17.

PART II

Chapter 4. The Doctrine of a Limited Brotherhood

1. See "Church News," *The Presbyterian Outlook,* March 17, 1952, p. 10.

2. *Ibid.*

3. *Ibid.*

4. *Op. cit.*

5. From a news item in *The Virginian* (Newport News, Va.), March, 1957.

6. Cf. Burrows, *An Outline of Biblical Theology,* p. 142.

7. *The Parables of Jesus* (New York: Harper & Bros., 1928), pp. 177-94.

8. *Ibid.,* p. 194.

9. News item in *The Christian Century,* May 22, 1957.

10. George A. Buttrick, "The Gospel According to St. Matthew," *The Interpreter's Bible,* VII, 304.

11. *Théologie du Nouveau Testament* (Paris: Editions Montaigne, 1951), p. 137: "La doctrine spécifiquement chrétienne était déja preparée par la théologie

biblique et juive: l'affirmation initiale sur l'homme crée à l'image de Dieu est un principe duquel se déduit la grandeur de la créature humaine: méconnaître sa dignité est injurier son Créateur; tous les hommes sont égaux, chacun a autant de valeur que la création tout entière."

12. So insists Clarence Tucker Craig, "The First Epistle to the Corinthians," *The Interpreter's Bible*, x, 79.

13. G. B. Stevens, *The Theology of the New Testament* (New York: Charles Scribner's Sons, 1899), pp. 119-20.

14. *Ibid.*

15. Burrows, *op. cit.*, p. 239.

16. Floyd V. Filson, *Jesus Christ the Risen Lord* (Nashville: Abingdon Press, 1956), p. 198.

17. *Op cit.*, p. 198. See the discussion in Theo Preiss, *Life in Christ*, tr. Harold Knight (London: SCM Press, 1954), pp. 34-35, of the meaning of "in Christ," "into Christ," and "in the Lord." Cf. C. A. A. Scott's brilliant treatment of the other Pauline terms for the Church, in *Christianity According to Saint Paul* (Cambridge: Cambridge University Press, 1939), pp. 150-69.

18. I hereby acknowledge my profound indebtedness to Preiss, *op. cit.*, pp. 32-42, for his suggestive analysis of the implications of Paul's advice to Philemon on questions of social ethics.

19. *Ibid.*, pp. 40-41.

20. *Ibid.*

21. Francis W. Beare, "The Epistle to the Colossians," *The Interpreter's Bible*, XI, 216.

22. Francis W. Beare, "The Epistle to the Ephesians," *The Interpreter's Bible*, X, 655.

23. *Ibid.*

24. V. 5. 2.

25. Quoted in Beare, "The Epistle to the Ephesians," p. 655.

26. *Seeking to Be Christian in Race Relations* (New York: Friendship Press, 1957), p. 13.

27. See Frederick Grant, *An Introduction to New Testament Thought* (Nashville: Abingdon Press, 1950), pp. 317-18.

28. Note Amos N. Wilder's discussion of Matt. 5:38-41 in *Eschatology and Ethics in the Teaching of Jesus* (New York: Harper & Bros., 1939), pp. 120-21.

Chapter 5. The Particularism of Jesus

1. Philip Mason, *Christianity and Race* (New York: St. Martin's Press, 1957), p. 103.

2. For a convenient summary of these, see Walter E. Bundy, *Jesus and the First Three Gospels* (Cambridge, Mass.: Harvard University Press, 1955), pp. 280-81.

3. See B. H. Streeter's discussion of the anti-Gentile attitude of the compiler of M, in *The Four Gospels* (New York: St. Martin's Press, 1951), pp. 511-16.

4. So H. L. Strack and P. Billerbeck, *Kommentar zum Neuen Testament aus*

Talmud und Midrasch, I (München: C. H. Beck'sche Verlagsbuchhandlung, 1922), pp. 724-25.

5. Buttrick, "The Gospel According to St. Matthew," p. 442.

6. See H. A. Guy, *A Critical Introduction to the Gospels* (New York: St. Martin's Press, 1955), p. 55.

7. *Op. cit.*, p. 157.

8. *Op. cit.*, p. 102.

9. *Ibid.*

10. *Op. cit.*, p. 17.

11. Rudolf Bultmann, *Die Geschichte der Synoptischen Tradition* (Göttingen: Vandenhoeck & Ruprecht, 1921), p. 151, contends for the origin of this disciplinary procedure in the Palestinian church.

12. *Op. cit.*, pp. 110-11.

Chapter 6. The Example of the Apostles

1. Howell, *op. cit.*, pp. 19-23.

2. *Op. cit.*, p. 13.

3. Dwight W. Culver, *Negro Segregation in the Methodist Church* (New Haven: Yale University Press, 1953), pp. 5 ff.

4. *Op. cit.* p. 147.

5. *Ibid.*, p. 152.

6. *Beginnings of the Christian Church* (New York: The Methodist Book Concern, 1929), p. 93.

7. W. A. Visser 'T Hooft, *The Ecumenical Movement and the Racial Problem* (Paris: UNESCO, 1954), p. 8.

8. *Ibid.*, p. 9.

9. (New York: Harper & Bro., 1944). Myrdal laments the gulf between the lofty democratic faith of American profession and the invidious discrimination of everyday practice.

10. George Foot Moore, *Judaism in the First Centuries of the Christian Era*, I (Cambridge, Mass.: Harvard University Press, 1932), 326-27.

11. *Ibid.*, p. 332.

12. *Ibid.*, p. 331.

13. See G. B. Caird, *The Apostolic Age* (London: Gerald Duckworth & Co., 1955), p. 29, who cites, as a second reason for the limited number of Jewish proselytes, the refusal of the Roman government to accord them the same rights and privileges which it granted those who were Jews by birth.

14. So suggests Henry J. Cadbury, *The Book of Acts in History* (London: A. & C. Black, 1955), p. 92.

15. Moore, *op. cit.*, pp. 323-24

16. *Mishnah*, "Niddah" IV. I.

17. So David Daube, *The New Testament and Rabbinic Judaism* (London: Athlone Press, 1956), p. 375.

18. John 4:9.

19. See Daube, *op. cit.*, pp. 373-82.

20. *Paul and Rabbinic Judaism* (London: S.P.C.K., 1948), p. 61.
21. Mishnah, "Demai" II. 3.
22. Bennett Harvie Branscomb, *Jesus and the Law of Moses* (New York: Richard R. Smith, 1930), p. 132, suggests that, while the term *hamartōloi* (sinners) does not apply exclusively to "individuals who merely disregarded . . . the ritual laws," in some instances the evangelists use it in this sense.
23. So *Ibid.*, p. 135.
24. *Ibid.*, p. 133.
25. H. A. A. Kennedy, *The Theology of the Epistles* (London: Gerald Duckworth & Co., Ltd., 1919), pp. 22 ff.
26. *Op. cit.*, p. 85.
27. "The Acts of the Apostles," *The Interpreter's Bible*, IX, 93.
28. Henry Cadbury, "The Hellenists," *The Beginnings of Christianity*, V, ed. F. J. Foakes-Jackson and Kirsopp Lake (New York: The Macmillan Co., 1933), pp. 59-73, defends the identification of Stephen's "Hellenists" as Gentiles.
29. Macgregor, *op. cit.*, p. 93.
30. Martin Dibelius, *Studies in the Acts of the Apostles*, ed. H. Greeven (New York: Charles Scribner's Sons, 1956), p. 122.
31. Floyd Filson, *Pioneers of the Primitive Church* (New York and Nashville: Abingdon-Cokesbury Press, 1940), p. 177.
32. Attested by Josephus, according to Origen, *Against Celsus* I. 47.
33. Filson, *Pioneers of the Primitive Church*, p. 177.
34. Eusebius, *Ecclesiastical History* III. 5. 2-3.
35. Filson, *Pioneers of the Primitive Church*, p. 179.
36. Branscomb, *op. cit.*, p. 2.

PART III

Introduction
1. (Chicago: The University of Chicago Press, 1955.)
2. Cf. Bright, *op. cit.*, p. 253, who declares that the New Testament answer to those who come to it asking. "What, then, ought we to do?" is quite simply this: "There shall no program be given you—except to be *the Church!*"
3. C. H. Dodd, *The Authority of the Bible* (London: James Nisbet & Co., 1928), pp. 207 ff., recognizes the strong sense of social solidarity among the Hebrews as the source of special difficulty for the early Christians.
4. H. H. Rowley, "The Authority of the Bible," *Encounter*, XVIII (Winter, 1957), 3.
5. "The Bible derives its authority from the Gospel," declares H. Cunliffe-Jones, *The Authority of the Biblical Revelation* (London: James Clarke & Co., 1945), p. 18.
6. Rowley, *op. cit.*, p. 11.

Chapter 7. The Character and Purpose of God
1. Bernhard W. Anderson, *The Unfolding Drama of the Bible* (New York: Association Press, 1957), pp. 14 ff.
2. Ludwig Köhler, *Theologie des Alten Testaments* (Tübingen: J. C. B.

Mohr, 1953), p. 71, notes: "Die Schöpfung ist, anders ausgedrückt, im AT nicht eine naturwissenschaftliche, sondern eine menschheitsgeschichtliche Aussage."

3. See G. Ernest Wright, The Challenge of Israel's Faith (University of Chicago Press, 1944).

4. Faith and History (New York: Charles Scribner's Sons, 1949), p. 36.

5. B. Davie Napier, From Faith to Faith (New York: Harper & Bros., 1955), p. 30.

6. Reinhold Niebuhr, op. cit., gives us a penetrating criticism of the philosophies of history which deny this view.

7. See Rudolf Bultmann, Theology of the New Testament, II, tr. Kendrick Grobel (New York: Charles Scribner's Sons, 1955), pp. 26-32.

8. See the brilliant discussion of this by C. H. Dodd in New Testament Studies (Manchester, Eng.: Manchester University Press, 1953), pp. 78 ff.

9. Paul S. Minear, Eyes of Faith (London: Lutterworth Press, 1948), p. 75, labels the "recognition of sin" as "the first step in a return . . . to the intended relationship to the Creator."

10. Divine and Human (London: The Epworth Press, 1952), p. 28.

11. Walther Eichrodt, Theologie des Alten Testaments, II (Leipzig: J. C. Hinrichs Verlag, 1935), pp. 49-50, credits the Old Testament writers with the attribution to the Creator of redemptive work in history.

12. A phrase used repeatedly by John Knox, On the Meaning of Christ (New York: Charles Scribner's Sons, 1947), to indicate the unity of the complex of factors that spawned the Church.

13. See Anderson, The Unfolding Drama of the Bible, p. 38.

14. Op. cit., p. 44.

15. Excerpts from my article "The Meaning of the Cross," Adult Teacher, IX (March, 1956), 4-5.

16. A book by D. M. Baillie (New York: Charles Scribner's Sons, 1948).

17. F. C. Grant, An Introduction to New Testament Thought (Nashville: Abingdon Press, 1950), p. 57.

18. Karl Barth, Dogmatics in Outline, tr. G. T. Thomson (London: SCM Press, 1949), p. 136, bridges this gap with this reminder: "The Judge who puts some on the left and others on the right, is in fact He who has yielded Himself to the judgment of God for me."

19. Otto J. Baab, The Theology of the Old Testament (Nashville: Abingdon Press, 1949), pp. 33-39.

20. See W. Arthur Faus, The Genius of the Prophets (New York and Nashville: Abingdon-Cokesbury Press, 1946), pp. 154 ff.

21. See his Leaves from the Notebook of a Tamed Cynic (New York: Willett, Clark & Co., 1929), pp. 113 ff.

22. Sherman E. Johnson, "The Gospel According to St. Matthew," The Interpreter's Bible, VII, 421.

23. Ibid.

24. George A. Buttrick, "The Gospel According to St. Matthew," *The Interpreter's Bible*, VII, 415.

25. Anderson, *The Unfolding Drama of the Bible*, p. 12.

26. Cf. C. H. Dodd, *The Bible To-day* (Cambridge, Eng.: Cambridge University Press, 1946), p. 130.

27. Napier, *op. cit.*, p. 205.

28. Dodd, *The Bible Today*, p. 131.

29. Köhler, *Theologie des Alten Testaments*, p. 17.

30. Paul Tillich, *Biblical Religion and the Search for Ultimate Reality* (University of Chicago Press, 1955), p. 45.

31. *Ibid.*

32. *Ibid.*

33. R. B. Y. Scott, *The Relevance of the Prophets* (New York: The Macmillan Co., 1944), p. 110.

34. *Ibid.*, pp. 107-8.

35. Wright, *op. cit.*, p. 28.

36. Anderson, *Understanding the Old Testament*, pp. 3-5.

37. A book by Roger L. Shinn (Philadelphia: The Westminster Press, 1957).

Chapter 8. The Dignity and Responsibility of Man

1. Merrimon Cuninggim, *Freedom's Holy Light* (New York: Harper & Bros., 1955), pp. 27-28.

2. The thesis of Reinhold Niebuhr's *The Children of Light and the Children of Darkness* (New York: Charles Scribner's Sons, 1944).

3. See the comments on this point in my book *The Conscience of Culture* (Nashville: The Board of Education of the Methodist Church, 1953). pp. 38-39.

4. See Reinhold Niebuhr, *Moral Man and Immoral Society: A Study in Ethics and Politics* (New York: Charles Scribner's Sons, 1932).

5. Cf. C. H. Dodd, *The Meaning of Paul for To-day* (London: Geo. Allen & Unwin, 1920), pp. 62-65.

6. J. Philip Hyatt, *Prophetic Religion* (Nashville: Abingdon Press, 1947), pp. 50-75.

7. Emil Brunner, *The Divine Imperative*, tr. Olive Wyon (Philadelphia: The Westminster Press, 1947), p. 404.

8. *Ibid.*

9. *Op. cit.*, II, 103.

10. See the treatment of this point in Amos Wilder, *Eschatology and Ethics in the Teaching of Jesus* (New York: Harper & Bros., 1950), pp. 125 ff.

11. Mason, *op. cit.*, p. 146.

12. *Ibid.*

Chapter 9. The Identity and Mission of the "Chosen People"

1. Gerald W. Broomfield, *The Chosen People* (New York: Longmans, Green & Co., 1954), p. 1.

2. "The Church shares with Christ," L. S. Thornton asserts in *The Common Life in the Body of Christ* (London: The Dacre Press, 1942), p. 55, "the whole vocation of the righteous Servant in suffering and sacrifice, death and victory."

3. See my article "The Birth of a Nation," *Christian Action*, IX (Fall, 1954), 3-5.

4. Paul Feine, *Theologie des Neuen Testaments* (Berlin: J. C. Hinrichs, 1953), p. 222, writes: "Die Versöhnung ist für den Apostel durchaus Gottes Werk am Menschen; der Mensch erfährt sie als etwas Passives. Auch darin steht sie in Parallele zur Rechfertigung."

5. Albert Gelin, *The Key Concepts of the Old Testament*, tr. George Lamb (New York: Sheed & Ward, 1955), p. 69.

6. Cf. Filson, *Jesus Christ the Risen Lord*, pp. 181 ff.

7. From a news item in *The Nashville Banner*, July 11, 1957.

8. A. M. Hunter, *Interpreting the New Testament, 1900-1950* (London: S.C.M. Press, 1951), pp. 135 ff.

9. A. M. Hunter, *The Unity of the New Testament* (London: SCM Press, 1943), pp. 46-74.

10. Walther Eichrodt, *Man in the Old Testament*, tr. K. and R. Gregor Smith (London; SCM Press, 1943), pp. 46-74.

11. Despite an element of exaggeration in his view, the words of Joseph Klausner, *The Messianic Idea in Israel*, tr. W. F. Stinespring (New York: The Macmillan Co., 1955), pp. 10-11, on this subject are basically right in emphasis: "The Jewish Messianic world . . . is idealistic and exalted, but it remains terrestrial. The Kingdom of Heaven of the Jewish Messiah is not only within the soul of man, but also upon the earth. . . . The Jewish people did not separate faith, which is spiritual, from social life, which is practical and political."

12. *Ibid.*, pp. 222-36.

13. The quoted phrases in this sentence are from Eichrodt, *Man in the Old Testament*, p. 77.

14. *Otherworldliness and the New Testament* (New York: Harper & Bros., 1954), p. 113.

15. *The Unity of the New Testament* (London: SCM Press, 1952), p. 106.

16. *Ibid.*, p. 86.

17. See Davies, *op. cit.*, pp. 54 ff.

18. Cf. the discussion by Thornton, *op. cit.*, p. 47.

19. Paul's phrase for the demonic forces which exploit man's debilitation to force his capitulation to the reign of sin.

20. Thornton, *op. cit.*, pp. 31 ff.

21. See Filson's discussion of this point, *Jesus Christ the Risen Lord*, pp. 221 ff.

22. Visser 'T Hooft, *op. cit.*, p. 65.

23. See Filson, *Jesus Christ the Risen Lord*, p. 221.

24. *Ibid.*, pp. 197-98.

25. *Ibid.*, p. 223.

26. See Hunter, *The Unity of the New Testament*, pp. 63-64.

INDEX OF SCRIPTURE

OLD TESTAMENT

INDEX

OF PERSONS AND SUBJECTS